IF SHE CAN ...

Inspiring Stories of Grit, Hope and Courage

Compiled by

Contributing Editor Katryna Johnson, J.D.

A Product of Mirelli Enterprises, Inc.

If She Can... Inspiring Stories of Grit, Hope and Courage

© 2019 by Mirelli Enterprises, Inc.

DISCLAIMER AND/OR LEGAL NOTICES

Printed in the United States of America

ISBN: 9781799116806

Table of Contents

Acknowledgements

This project would not have been possible without the assistance of so many people.

Thank you to Michelle Bryant-Griffin for a terrific cover design.

Thank you to Timothy Eberly on Unsplash for the beautiful warrior princess photograph.

Thank you "Eagle Eye" editor Ann Beauchamp.

Thank you to all our terrific contributors:
Ann Beauchamp, Dr. Ja'net Bishop, Tianca Breedlove, Michelle Bryant-Griffin, Dr. Elizabeth Castle, JL Coston, Lynn DelGaudio, Keisha Hawes, Camilla Herold, Demetria Johnson, Katryna Johnson, J.D., Mary Johnson, Kimberly Mills, Chrissy Mullins, Robin Nazon, and Iskra Perez-Salcedo.

Thank you to all the participants of the Mirelli Raising the Bar Mastermind group for your ideas, encouragement and support.

Forward

Child abuse. Poverty. Domestic Violence. Miscarriage. Foster Care. Health Issues. Bad Boss. Broken relationships. Grief. Feeling lost, confused, inadequate, and alone.

Every woman has a story. They are all familiar tales and yet foreign at the same time.

When I first started this project, I wasn't sure what types of stories women would want to share. As the stories came in, they were raw and real. I was more and more amazed. Who are these women? Where did they get their strength? How did I end up with these terrific women in my circle? How many of the women I see every day have these incredible stories of their past? How many are struggling with something today and need to hear from someone who has been there?

Who will benefit from a story in this book?

I have spent time with many of these ladies in a variety of situations and rarely had a clue of what they had gone through. At one point, I was reading a story submission and thought, "Who the heck went through all of this?" and when I looked at the author, I was shocked. I have known her for over four years and had no idea.

One of the many things these women have in common is their ability to accept what happened and move forward in a positive, uplifting manner. They truly acted with Grit, Hope, and Courage and live their lives openly and unashamed of their past.

5

Forward

They all have a heart to help other women by sharing their stories and want the world to be a better place.

But one thing stood out to me as I read their stories: God. Their faith and reliance on Him is credited for many of their triumphs. Listening to His voice and leaning on His promises made a difference.

I am honored that every woman stepped forward and was willing to share their story. I am so privileged to know them and celebrate them.

There's a meme I see frequently that says "Everyone you meet is struggling with something. Be kind always."

My hope is that you will be encouraged and inspired by the stories we have collected.

If She Can ... you can, too.

Katryna Johnson

Contributing Editor
Owner, Mirelli Enterprises, Inc.

I Smiled Through My Pain as I Found a Way to Heal

In 1992 I was 12 years old and loving life. I was becoming a teenager and doing things that pre-teens did, such as listening to music, having boyfriends, and hanging out with friends. As most teens do, I didn't have a care in the world. Then one day my innocence was ripped away from me. It came so suddenly, like a thief in the night. I was no longer a pre-teen living her best life. I was violated, and it was the beginning of a world of sadness and pain.

I was only 12. I was touched and made to touch in a way that no woman or man should ever be touched at that age or any age until they are ready. I had no idea what had happened. I had no choice. I never asked for it nor did I want it to happen. It just did, and I had no control in it. I was told to never say anything because no one would believe me. I was told I would never be anything and that I actually wanted it to happen. He told me that no man would ever love me.

I honestly believed what he said. I believed it for many reasons but the main reason I thought it was true (and that still haunts me to this day) is that, as I was coming into my womanhood I had feelings inside. I was interested in the feelings I was feeling at that time. When I was told that I "wanted it," in the back of my mind I wondered if that was true. I know now that the feelings I was having were not supposed to be in that atmosphere. It was supposed to be with someone I was attracted to, someone close to my age, someone who I chose to have these sexual feelings for. I was robbed of this. I was given no choice in who I had my first hormonal experience with and that affected me, and it affected me badly.

I had to keep silent about what had happened to me. I had to deal with not understanding why it happened. I had to cope without knowing what I had to do to move on in my life without telling anyone. This was the first major milestone in my life and I had no idea the magnitude of what had just happened.

I tried to block it out and forget it. That didn't work. I then decided to blame myself so that I didn't have to face the fact I was violated, and unfortunately that did work. I carried this guilt and shame silently for many years, and thinking it was all my fault made it easier to keep silent.

Even being in this person's presence after it happened was horrifying for me. But no one knew but him and me and I had to keep it that way.

Shortly after this happened I became a woman and started my cycle. I was so scared because I thought I had gotten a disease or worse. I had to tell my mom but didn't know what she would say. I told her I was having an issue and she gave me that talk. I wanted to tell her what happened but couldn't bring the words to my mouth. I let it go.

A couple years passed, and I was trying to move on in my life. That was difficult because I was so afraid of men, my brothers, my dad, any male. But I had to try to bury those feelings because no one could know what happened. I don't know how to this day I was able to hide it. But I did. I would see this person often and it disgusted me every time. I just walked away and tried to be as far away from him as possible.

I just wished I could have said something. What if some other girl was getting violated like me? What if he did worse to someone else? Was I the first one? So many thoughts ran through my head time after time, year after year. But still I remained silent.

During this time my dad passed away, so I had something to take my mind off being molested. I was heartbroken and confused and angry with how my life at only 14 years could be so horrible.

Thoughts crossed my head of leaving this world, but I never planned anything, and I knew I could never do something like that. But to say that it didn't cross my mind would be a lie.

My mom was my everything after my dad was gone. She comforted me, she loved on me, and she prayed for me, even though she did not know what all her daughter was going through.

I was broken.

I maintained and tried to start living and having fun again. I surrounded myself with friends and just tried to forget. Every time I did forget for a time, it would pop back up in my thoughts again. I just couldn't get over it.

My cousin and one of my best friends were over hanging out with me and we decided to play a game where we told each other our deepest secret. We all shared but my secret was so deep it shocked my cousin

9

and friend. They had no idea but for some reason I just had to let it out. No more could I keep it in. I was so relieved when I let it out. A ton of weight came out of my body just by saying it. Part of the game was to swear to secrecy and never tell a soul. However, because of the magnitude of what happened and the fact they knew I still saw this person from time to time, they forced me to go upstairs and tell my mom. That turned out to be the hardest thing I had to do. She was devastated, angry, sad, disappointed but happy I told her, so she could now protect me. I had been protecting myself for four years and she was so hurt.

She immediately took steps to make sure I would never be around him. She had to tell a few people for this to happen but didn't want too many people to know.

I can't imagine what my mom was going through, how she was feeling. I hated she had to deal with this. She was already suffering from kidney failure and I felt I was adding more pressure, sadness and pain to her. She sought help for me through counseling, church, and legal help.

Unfortunately, no legal action could be taking because the statute of limitations had run out and he didn't rape me so there was no proof of what had happened. This angered my mom. She wished I would have said something sooner.

I don't know the conversations my mom may have had with my brothers or if she had even told all of them. I do know she told one of my brothers. I think she felt that she had to take on the burden because of her unconditional love for me. She didn't want me to have to carry the burden by myself. A mother's love is unmeasurable. I always felt protected with my mom, but I know that she felt some sort of guilt.

After I told my mom and the shock wore off, I started counseling. Counseling in the black community has always been taboo, something that was looked down on. Still to this day I have no idea as to why, but I am so grateful that my mom took the steps and had me speak to someone.

Counseling helped change my life. It helped to mold me into a different person. It helped me to stop feeling guilty and embarrassed. It took time, but I eventually realized I was still the same girl I thought I had lost. Counseling helped to build up my self-esteem and confidence. It helped me to understand my worth. Because of counseling, I was able to rebuild my life and reclaim my innocence, my happiness and my confidence. I started to realize how incredibly strong I was at such a young age. I felt I could go through anything.

Counseling didn't stop once I became an adult, either. I started to have some of the same feelings I had as a child again, not feeling worthy, being extremely submissive to men, attracted to older men, and other unhealthy feelings. Mainly I started using my sexual nature to try to find love and affection but waking up the morning after feeling disgusting and unworthy. My emotions started spiraling out of control but this time I used other things to cope with my feelings like drugs, alcohol and sex. I needed a fix. I needed to get myself back under control.

I ran back to counseling and had to start my process all over again. This time it was different. It was more intense, more crying and more stories to tell. I eventually had to learn how to forgive myself and understand that I was more than these destructive behaviors. I deserve more and came to understand that I require and demand respect. I had to learn how to respect myself and demand myself to want more. After a few years I learned the true meaning of forgiveness. It's a very powerful thing to have to do.

I had been given this task by God to help others who may not have the resources I did to get help to overcome the shame and guilt. I learned that I had to forgive my attacker and I did. I absolutely forgive this horrible human being for what he did. I had to for my peace and to regain power back in my life.

Now I can help people like myself get their power back.

I realize that my attacker -- no matter the money he has, the adventures he has taken in life and the happiness he thinks he has -- his life can never amount to the strength I have. He can never have total peace, and he will never be able to live his life in truth and honesty. He will always know what he did, and he must live with that.

So I'm free, I'm strong and I overcame!

Can he say the same?

This is my #Metoo!

ABOUT THE AUTHOR

Kimberly Mills is a true warrior who has walked through the trenches of pain and grief many times. Her resilience is admirable. When you speak with her, you cannot help but be in awe of her strength and courage. She is an entrepreneur with her own travel agency and an author.

In her book, ***My Truth: Enduring Death on Many Levels***, she recounts several moving experiences, including the pain of becoming parentless by the age of eighteen. Her book is available via Amazon.

Her purpose and passion are to help others overcome the pain in their lives, especially their grief at losing a loved one. She is associated with local organizations that provide grief counseling and services to children who have lost both parents. She hopes to branch out into speaking on the topics of death and grief soon.

To contact Kimberly for speaking engagements, email her at kimmills2012@gmail.com

Find her on Facebook: Author Kimberly Mills

To learn more about Timeless Travelz, visit
http://myvortex365.com/timelesstravelz

I am Divinely Operating
Purposefully Everyday

The happy face I wore disguised the ugliest tormented soul. I was often referred to as the "strong one." What others didn't realize was that I learned at an early age how to show my ego rather than my soul. I hid my heartaches.

I was born to two runaway teenagers who couldn't have possibly known what was best for another little being. My paternal grandparents helped to raise me. I have my grandparents to thank for instilling biblical truths into me at a very young age. No matter what I endured I always felt things could have been worst and knew God was always watching over me.

I would later discover I knew the ways of God but I didn't know the How and the Why. I didn't know God for myself. After having such a loving experience with them, the rest of my childhood was nothing short of traumatic. I went through life holding the image of my grandparent's loving household in my mind as the perfect family unit.

Once I moved from their house, life became extremely challenging. I would spend a few months at one family member's house and a year at a different family member's house. During my childhood I witnessed and experienced abusive behavior. Unfortunately, as a young girl I was introduced to the lustful ways of the world.

15

The positive of moving from house to house was the opportunity it gave me to experience different lifestyles. I experienced life with some who didn't have much financially yet they somehow kept it all together for their family. I experienced life with others who didn't have many financial worries (I mean you could eat and drink anything you wanted and not get yelled at for it) and I experienced life with a few people who were living hardship to hardship due to their struggle with drugs.

What I witnessed as a child was my motivation as a young adult to achieve financial security. I felt this would bring me a sense of freedom. During my twenties I was a self-employed Private Duty Caregiver averaging $50,000 a year. In my early twenties I was a signed model for a local Baltimore agency. In my mid-twenties I owned and operated an entertainment model agency and in my later twenties (soon after I met the guy who would change the course of my life) I graduated cosmetology school. I pursued these ventures all while continuing to make a living as a Private Duty Caregiver.

I was never one to allow the pitfalls of life to stop me from what I wanted to achieve. I was content with life because of my accomplishments but I didn't feel complete. I traveled as I wanted, fed my expensive love for food (huge deal for me, food is life), shopped as I wanted and had bi-weekly hair and nail salon appointments. I had money to pay bills without a worry, money saved and money to spend. I was the person who friends and family knew they could always depend on in a time of need. At the age of 29 I could honestly say I had created the life I wanted for myself.

I still longed to have the loving family unit I had always held in my mind. I would soon meet the guy who I thought was created just perfect for me. He very quickly became my partner in everything. We were inseparable.

Early in our relationship, some members of my family voiced that they didn't feel he was the one for me and they began to distance themselves from us. At the time this didn't bother me because everything else in my life was as I wanted it to be and NOW... I had my guy (the missing link). That was all that mattered.

More than anything he made me feel wanted. In hindsight, there were signs everyday showing that I should break up with him. However, I was an adult who operated from a place of childhood brokenness, my coping mechanisms didn't allow for me to see the red flags as others saw them.

What one person saw as a negative trait, I saw as a chance to help another person experience the gift of unconditional love. I felt if I loved him unconditionally, he would see the error of his ways. Reality was I could never truly love him. I never unconditionally, wholeheartedly loved the core of who I was. In my need to love his flaws, was really the desire to have someone love me out of the bondage of past pain and disappointments.

At the time I met this guy, my standards were so shallow. I wanted a physically attractive fella, who was tall with a nice physique. I also needed to be able to have good times and lots of laughs with my guy. In the beginning he was all of that! What was hidden was that he was a liar, cheater, an alcoholic and an abusive person. He hadn't any real connection with his own family and he eventually succeeded at having me isolated from those whom I was once very close.

During my pregnancy my eyes began to open to those traits mentioned before as the negatives that they were. Yet, I chose to marry this man simply because I was still chasing the "family image" that I held in my mind. He was my complete opposite and totally not what I wanted to be my forever or a role model for my unborn child. My shallowness landed me a shallow individual with whom I eventually shared a very shallow marriage.

During the marriage, I not only dealt with the abuse from my husband, but life began to knock me around as well. Each child I birthed had trauma after they were born. My first was born with a hole in his heart and my second was found unresponsive at 5 weeks (both healthy now). Life at this point had completely beaten me down to someone who was merely existing and thus began the downhill spiral into a dark hole. I had also allowed myself to be spiritually shutdown trying to please the man I married.

It didn't happen overnight. This attack was very subtle. My husband voiced he wanted to find another church home because the Bishop was hard for him to understand. We visited a few churches then stopped going altogether. Before I realized it, I was far removed from God. I was just a shell floating day to day. I felt completely empty and alone. I was very aware of my reality yet, I didn't know where to begin to turn things around for the better. Silently I was tucking all of those "new" disappointments deep down inside of me, along with the old childhood trauma. I looked as if I was holding myself together, but I felt the weight of my hasty choices. I was physically in pain every single day due to stress.

After three years of ups and downs with this man, one late night our two children bore witness to their mother being dragged by her hair, choked and punched. This was not my first incident with my husband. However, this was the first time I had ever experienced a gut feeling telling me that if I didn't find a way out, I was going to be killed.

After that incident we became estranged, but he still found ways to continue with his abuse. He took it upon himself to expose nude pictures of me for family members, co-workers, friends and physicians that I work with to view.

I must say, repairing oneself mentally and emotionally is the hardest task for anyone to ever take on. The worst part of my whole ordeal was trying my best to put my broken pieces together while still being the best mom possible for my two boys. Although I was finally breathing fresh air because I was out of that toxic environment, I now faced the harsh realities of being in a position that I fought so hard not to be in and with the added responsibility of raising my children. The lifestyle that I once worked so hard to build for myself was now just a memory.

While I found employment that offered stability, great benefits and potential to progress within the company, I took a significant pay cut and then daycare took most of what I did make. I began reaching out to a few family members for a helping hand or even a place to stay. Pleas for help fell on deaf ears. Although hurtful at the time, I would later find that God needed me to ONLY depend on him.

I could no longer afford to live in the affluent neighborhood I had once chosen for my family. So, I moved us to a neighborhood that was considered low income housing. I could no longer afford my vehicle, so it was repossessed. I was on WIC (and needed everything that they offered), I received food stamps and used any other government assistance programs that my low income qualified me to receive.

Mentally, I fell into the darkest hole I had ever experienced. I was completely beat down by my circumstances. There were times that all I could do was cry but God knows our hearts. My tears were accepted as if they were prayers. Even in my darkest days I was sure to say "Thank You Lord" because I knew things could have been worst.

To my surprise turning a blind eye to my troubles didn't come easy this time. I was lacking the confidence I once had for life itself and my self-esteem was depleted. I began to look for comfort in men. When meeting a guy, I would always share pictures or stories of my happier days. Those old pictures and stories became gentle reminders of the fearlessness I once had pertaining to life. Little by little my confidence and self-esteem began to grow.

After several failed attempts at any sort of meaningful relationship, I had to remind myself that I was already dealing with enough and there was no way I should allow another person to add to the damages that were already consuming my life.

I kept telling myself THIS IS NOT MY LIFE. I knew this struggle was not what I wanted for myself or my children. I felt I had begun to allow life to just happen to me, rather than creating my life as I once had. I began to shift my focus from finding the right man to rebuilding myself from poverty and depression. Giving my children a childhood that they wouldn't have to recover from once they were adults became my greatest motivation. My focus now was to pour my all into my children while furthering my career.

The man I once viewed as my perfect guy I now felt was pure evil, the devil himself. During this time, I was blaming my estranged husband for my setback. This way of thinking resulted in me spending a year being engulfed with negative thoughts of failure and unworthiness. Those negative thoughts ultimately kept me stuck in the very dark place I didn't want to be. Praying was something I felt I had forgotten how to do.

However, due to a series of events, the realization that God was calling me closer to him led me back into prayer mode. By praying and reconnecting with the source, it became evident that I was right where I was supposed to be.

I was so beat down and drained that no amount of sleep could revive me. It was revealed to me that my soul was tired. Solitude was needed so I could do my soul work. It was time to go beyond the surface of what was seen for self-discovery and deep self-reflection from years of abuse. I had to accept that no one would be able to "save" me except me. Rather than being fixated on the storm, I became focused on the fact that God had purposely isolated me from the world and I needed to discover what exactly it was He was trying to tell me.

This is when my thoughts shifted from negatively thinking I'm broken and helpless to positively knowing I'm going to grow through this experience and heal. I went from asking, "Why is this my life?" to asking, "How did this become my life?" It was time for me to dig deep into my murky past so that I could began to heal and become whole. Without much money and no one around, I was forced to sit and deal with the reality of what my life had become which was poverty, depression and hopelessness.

God showed me a preview of what my life could be if I just remained obedient to Him. After seeing a brighter life for myself and my children, all hope was renewed. I knew that if I became comfortable with the current situation, then I would be continuing the same cycle for my children. From generation to generation this cycle would continue until someone was ready to heal. I chose to be that person to end the cycle. I began to speak life back into myself. Spending time with God put my whole situation into perspective. It wasn't the end for me. It was the beginning. I could allow the little girl inside of my adult body to be healed. It was time I gave my younger self closure and grew into the woman I was always meant to become.

Now would come the toughest battle I had ever faced, the healing process. It would be raw and real, something I had never been with myself. I had to get to the truth of what was keeping me tied to the childhood trauma for all those years (I had to work through layers). I had to ask myself, how did I truly feel about it (which usually was met with an array of different emotions). I needed to understand what tricks I used throughout the years that allowed the trauma to stay concealed within me. This is when I learned that the old saying "time heals all wounds," was false. The healer of all wounds is the love of God.

Going through the most difficult time of my life, I knew I needed to surrender myself to the will of God and allow him to work on me. A huge component of allowing God to work on me during the midst my darkest storm was to stop dating and deciding to abstain from Sacred Energy Xchange (sexual behaviors). That decision created a commitment to my spiritual being. This has given me time to grow closer to God by getting to know Him within myself. One must understand that no matter how deep the issue is and no matter how long you have struggled with it, you can absolutely heal from any trauma, become whole and live in complete freedom of being authentically you. It doesn't mean that those things never took place. It means the trauma no longer controls your life.

I was not at all prepared for the internal battle I would face. In the end it would prove to be all necessary. Initially, I repented from my sinful behavior and continually asked God to renew my mind. I had to learn how to forgive those who may never ask for my forgiveness. I also had to learn how to forgive myself.

There were times I thought it would be much easier to go back to my old self but then I would be given a vision of our future. I knew reverting backwards wouldn't be worth it. I couldn't fathom the thought of my children having to live as survivors in the cycle of hopelessness because of my choices.

True healing is a process that results in growth and it doesn't happen overnight. This is how I learned the importance of patiently waiting and most importantly how I conducted myself during the wait. Even when I could not make sense of the plan. I made the decision to exercise my faith, trusting in the unseen, including God's timing. A great example is, although at my job I am administrative personnel, I was nominated to be trained as a health and wellness coach. It was during this training that I was given the tools to sincerely forgive my estranged husband. This is when I knew everything I was experiencing was working for a greater plan. I decided there was no other way but to stay committed to and consistent for God.

By grabbing ahold of each lesson and taking the lessons with me to the next season of my life, I was prepared for the next test. Once I became aware of the spiritual warfare that was happening, I was able to recognize the tricks of the enemy. This was the time that I used my God-given inner strength to persevere past the enemy and into my winning season. When the tests came and Oooh! did they come, I knew not to respond with the same answers as I did in the past. That is where I began to see my growth. I didn't want to continue to get the same out of life which would only be recycled experiences. Being stuck in a cycle of dysfunction, confusion and unhappiness couldn't bring me joy.

My unforeseen situation of poverty and depression turned out to be the set up for a needed spiritual journey to heal and become whole. Everything that was taken away from me was only to bless me with a deeper understanding of life. I used what I learned in the darkness as tools to grow and keep moving closer to the light.

My sense of freedom now comes from being able to live authentic to who I am. Being obedient to God has allowed my physical to align with my spiritual. Let me share with you there is no way I would ever go back to the way things used to be. During my journey it has been as if God himself has held out his hand for me to grab ahold of and He has walked me out of my darkness into a brighter life. I have joy that does not depend on a person, place, situation or thing. I am excelling in my career at the Department of Veterans Affairs faster than I could have ever expected. I know God himself is to thank for everything.

What people don't realize is He will have people already in place for you to succeed before you even get to your destination. He will speak to the hearts of others on your behalf. Before making decisions, I talk with God through prayer, and allow the answers to come. No one would ever be able to convince me that prayer doesn't work. The part that most forget is that although we pray, we must still do our part. God will give us instructions, we must follow those instructions to get to where he is trying to take us.

My life has become proof of my faith. When others began to comment on the positivity they noticed without them ever knowing I was working to heal myself, I knew the light within could no longer be contained. Rather than being an extension of my years of darkness, my children have become an extension of my light. My healing is changing the course of their lives as well as generations to come. Through all that I've gone through things could've turned out differently but GOD! HE KEPT MY MIND!!! I always knew I was better than my entire situation. It took two long dark years for me to discover and accept my true worth.

I emerged out of the darkness having a deeper appreciation for loving myself. I am mindful of my everyday choices and the components that work together to keep me balanced emotionally, spiritually, mentally, physically and even socially. That is the ultimate self-care. It has only been a year of me surrendering and becoming obedient to God, so I haven't achieved all that has been shown to me. Sometimes I find myself looking back in amazement of how far I've come out of the valley. I am staying present during the journey while I reach my God-ordained destination.

I plan to use my God-given wings to soar with the purpose of helping others to see that they, too, can heal from brokenness. The journey of healing and becoming whole looks different for everyone. The only thing that is the same is that it's not easy by any means but well worth every tear. Allow those tears to water the seeds for your future.

ABOUT THE AUTHOR

 Tianca Inez Breedlove is a visionary mother raising her children with the understanding that they will pass their life lessons and experiences to the generations to come. She is extremely

passionate about living authentic to who she is called to be and empowering others to become reacquainted with their true identities before trauma, hurt, pain and disappointment took place. By day she works for the Department of Veterans Affairs as a Lead Medical Support Assistant as well as a Whole Health Coach. However, she encourages others daily through multiple social media sites one being her Facebook group Beyond the Surface.

She is a certified Christian Life Coach with a focus on teaching others the importance of understanding what is in the Bible and applying what is written daily as a tool for a purposeful life. She is working on a book, seeking speaking opportunities and is also accepting new clients.

Her belief in God was magnified in the darkest hour when she began to seek more of Him and he continuously showed himself to be true. Currently living in Baltimore, MD with her two children she is now living according to God's promises. ***

Ms. Breedlove can be reached by email Keepersofthenext@gmail.com, IG breedlove_ladytee and or Facebook at Tianca Breedlove

I Chose to Change

Did you ever walk into a room full of people with groups standing around chatting and feel totally out of place? How demeaning to wander around, hovering on the periphery of various clusters of people, having absolutely nothing to say to participate in the conversation. I felt like a total misfit, "What's wrong with me?" Couple that with feeling like nothing I did was ever good enough and you have a big roadblock to ever being confident enough to run a business.

During my high school years, while the other girls rode their horses, trail riding and chattering away, I spent my time in the stable braiding horses' manes and tails to earn my entry fees for horse shows. I loved to dance, but what guy wanted to dance with a girl who couldn't even carry on a conversation. I was just not social. I didn't even get invited to my senior prom.

When I looked at the facts of my life, I didn't see why I was struggling so much. I was always an over achiever, graduated near the top of my high school graduating class, the first girl to take Advanced Mathematics in that very large school. I graduated at the top of my class as an X-ray technician when that curriculum was practicum from day one. Late in life, I graduated at the top of my class at College of Charleston in Computer Information Systems, almost unheard of for someone to graduate from the Computer Science department with a 4.0 GPA.

So, what's this roadblock with talking to people and why do I feel so inadequate?

The first step for me was listening to my very best friend and sister whom I adopted, Pat McPherson. She helped me begin to live out Romans 8:1 "For now there is no condemnation for those who are in Christ Jesus." We are our own worst critic, and when we feel like we're just not good enough and always trying to please others, we beat up on ourselves. As a Christian, I knew I had a heavenly Father, but I had not been applying His truths and promises in my life.

Once I began to read the promises in the Scriptures about how we're made in the image of God and we have the mind of Christ, I began to trust Him more and my confidence began to grow in small ways. I repeated Romans 8:1 over and over, and it began to take root. I began to accept myself just the way I was. Little by little I began to accept that neither I nor anyone else is perfect, but that doesn't mean we're not OK. We each have our own gifts and strengths, mine were just more introspective.

The next step was like turning the light on! While I rarely attend Women's Center events, I found myself in a room full of about 100 people, both men and women. The session was led by Cathy Liska, Guide from the Side®. She asked us a series of questions and explained scoring. Based on our results, she then divided us into groups in the 4 corners of the room with some very specific questions to answer collaboratively. Wow, my group only had 4 people and the other 96ish were about evenly disbursed.

Each group shared things like:
- What do you want other people to know about you?
- What do you dislike about how people treat you?
- How do you want to be treated?

When she got to our group so we could share our answers, she told why we only had 4 people in the group even though we made up about 35% of the population. We are passive and logical, and many of us are introverts. The individuals in other groups either enjoy people and interaction, some just want to cut to the chase to get things done, or support others and are nurturers. Because of our preferences, we are often the folks who avoid large gatherings. We are happy spending time alone and may appear to be unsociable, so it takes encouragement for us to be included.

After the session was over, lots of people from the other groups came over to talk with us. "No wonder my wife reacts like that!" one gentleman said. Others said they will be more mindful of people who seem unsociable but really are friendly when you take the time to have a one-on-one conversation and get to know them.

What an eye opener! Cathy introduced me to a book called "**_Quiet, The Power of Introverts in a World that Can't Stop Talking_**" by Susan Cain. Susan also has a Ted Talk on YouTube. I'm not weird or a misfit! I can now appreciate and embrace life the way God made me. How freeing!

Next came a different kind of "education" – retraining my brain, shining that light into the deep places! A lot of people seemed to have coaches, so I asked a friend for a suggestion about who would be a good coach. Instead of pointing me to a business coach, she suggested a semi-retired Lutheran pastor, Rod Ronneberg.

Being a Christian and familiar with ministry for healing of memories and childhood issues, I had two questions for Pastor Rod before I would open my innermost thoughts to him. First, I needed to know his theology is based on Orthodox Biblical Christianity. Second, I needed to know if he had experience with spiritual warfare, knowing "Our battle is not with flesh and blood but …. with the spiritual forces of wickedness…" Eph. 6:12. If I'm going to allow someone to expose things in my life and root them out, I want to know where his wisdom comes from and what weapons he has at his disposal. Our enemy, the devil, will try everything to keep us down and sneaks in like a thief in the night.

Pastor Rod and I spent about 3 months going through material called "*__Life Mastery__*" by Mark Fournier. Each section was long, with many probing questions and exercises. As I look back over the various sessions, I see how masterfully this material helps replace self-destructive thought processes with healthy thought processes that reformulated the way we approach life and our perception about different things we encounter. I had often joked about wanting a brain re-wire job, and that's exactly what I got.

This mindset shift was critical because my life was about to change in a big way. After 35 years in the public accounting arena, I was thrust into a hard choice to start my own business. Though I had considered that for a while, that feeling of insecurity made me scared to death to put myself out there. But sometimes the Lord opens a door wide and even backs it up with a swift kick you-know-where. So, in 2007, I went from employee to business owner overnight. Fortunately, He gave me a soft landing. The CPA I had worked with for 30 years gave me all my clients. He even wrote letters of recommendation for me. So, I started with a solid business and great clients, yet I was petrified at the idea of finding new clients.

Enter Dianne Shaver. We had met previously through networking groups I had reluctantly attended. When the time was right, Dianne and I both knew we should work together. Dianne is a seasoned coach helping me work through my insecurities and try to figure out what I want to be when I grow up. After failing at a couple of different ancillary business ventures and with Dianne's guidance, I've come back to my roots in the accounting arena, which is where I feel most at home.

More than anything, Dianne has helped me realize just how capable I really am. She has also helped me learn that everyone is afraid when they begin to grow, everyone fails, everyone comes to forks in the road and makes changes in their life and business.

I'm opening my eyes to new opportunities and areas of focus to expand my business. Dianne has held several events called "What's the Big Idea?" and teaches people how to pitch their ideas before a panel of investors. I've pitched a process called DataMash Connect before a panel of investors and now have a registered trademark for that process. That grew out of personal observation of how businesses waste time and money entering the same information in more than one system in their accounting, which is redundant and error prone. I would never had taken that on even as recently as three years ago. I've recently re-branded myself as a Business Accounting Detective. I look for and make corrections in the accounting records for accurate interim reporting and to minimize fees for tax preparation. I'm also adding implementation of internal accounting controls and best practices to my services since the absence of controls increases vulnerability to loss and theft.

For an extra touch of God's humor, Dianne has been a professional ballet dancer and has danced ballroom, which is my extracurricular passion. She helps me push through struggles with dancing, as well as business and just life.

And I still have my fingers in other business interests that fit who I am. I am now on the Board of Directors of a privately held oil and gas company, thanks to becoming friends with a gentleman I met through one of my failed business ventures. Interesting how seeming failure can change the course of your life. I have an ownership interest in a company called RSL Holdings, which builds affordable housing communities with an unusual twist. I am a close associate of a nutritional researcher and the owners of Veterans Technology Systems (VTS), a veteran owned technology applications and development company developing a highly sophisticated mobile "POD" that can be adapted to everything from a mobile laboratory for the poultry industry to school and border security.

Today, what once was a wall called introversion keeps coming down one brick at a time. I look forward to networking opportunities and the new people I'm meeting. Instead of hovering on the periphery of groups of people chatting, now I look for those standing by themselves and go up to them. I've met some wonderful people that way and had some amazing conversations! Yes, I am still an introvert. I love times when I can be home by myself with a lengthy project or a good movie. However, I am also excited when that mischievous gal inside me comes out to play.

I know that I am fearfully and wonderfully made, knit in my mother's womb before the beginning of time by my loving heavenly Father. He has made me unique and given me all I need for those things He has called me to do.

Each person has their own challenges to overcome. My prayer is that you will be encouraged to listen to that still small voice inside to guide and direct your footsteps, one step at a time. Be encouraged to have the patience to wait, even do nothing. It's amazing the wisdom that comes in the quiet moments.

If I had one piece of advice for anyone reading this, it would be to take a chance. We're not meant to walk through life alone. Find people to come along side you. Those people may be business coaches, life coaches, close friends or a combination of several people. Know that your support group will likely change over time as you change. Don't be afraid … make your decision to grow. You are not a misfit. You are a child of God.

ABOUT THE AUTHOR

Originally from Augusta, GA, Ann Beauchamp holds a bachelor's degree in Computer Information Systems from the College of Charleston (SC), graduating at the top of her class. She worked in the Certified Public Accounting arena for over 35 years where she had numerous engagements teaching clients accounting and bookkeeping skills as well as installing and configuring their accounting software. Since 2007, she has operated her own business accounting and software consulting company. She works with a variety of small and medium sized businesses helping them with various business accounting needs. She loves helping her clients understand their accounting functions and financial statements. One of her favorite phrases is "It's not rocket science!" and then she proceeds to prove it.

She is a member of SC Christian Chamber of Commerce, Mirelli Entrepreneur Training for Women, West Ashley

James Island Business Association, attends God in the Workplace, LifeWorks, 1Million Cups, North Charleston Chamber of Commerce events, and numerous other events in the business community.

Ann rode horses in her early years, participating in horse shows and fox hunts. Her current extracurricular passion is competitive ballroom dancing, though you will also find her having fun social dancing. Thus she named her company HorseDancer Business Consulting. She conducted small church choirs for many years, currently sings in the choir at St. Michaels Anglican Church, and occasionally in the Charleston Symphony Orchestra Chorus when her dance schedule permits. She is a volunteer for the Red Cross serving on the Disaster Services Team.

You can find out more about Ann and her business at:
https://HorseDancerConsulting.com/
https://www.linkedin.com/in/AnnBeauchamp/
You can contact her at (843) 639-6090 or
Ann@HorseDancerConsulting.com

I Redesigned My Mind for
Remarkable Results

July 2014, a beautiful warm, sunny, spectacular North Carolina day. I had just finished a great 7-mile run, and I was enjoying the high endorphin levels. This was a particularly good run. My form and strides were on point. My breathing perfect and relaxed. My body felt great. Strong. Steady. Conditioned. Muscular. I was so grateful to be in such good running shape, and although a great workout, running was also always extremely meditative for me. During my runs is when much of my creativity and insights would be expressed, and all my stress released.

This sunny July day, I was feeling so good, I decided I wanted to continue my workout in some way before taking my pooch for a walk in the nearby park. It was only noon and I had the entire afternoon ahead of me. I had nowhere to be, no work to do and I was high on dopamine, norepinephrine, serotonin, and as mentioned, endorphins were also elevated. I was feeling high on life. Best day ever!

I was looking forward to the four-day July 4th holiday weekend and the great weather that the forecast was proposing. I was also looking forward to a trip to Connecticut the following week to see my family. It had been eight years since I had seen them and was so excited for the long overdue reunion. I was having such a great day and was eagerly anticipating the events of the coming days and weeks.

I decided to lift some weights before taking my pooch for a walk. The community where I lived had a fitness center, so I headed over. I started with some behind the neck lat pull downs. I was strong; I was pulling 70-80 pounds on a given day at that time. I began: one... two... blank.

In an instant, everything changed. I don't know if I finished the second pull, or if I had three or four pulls or more. I don't remember much except that I felt something snap and the bar came screeching down on my head with the force of 70-80 pounds. Upon impact, I literally felt my brain shake like a Christmas snow globe inside my head, swishing back and forth, and I saw a flash. I lifted my hand to feel my head and found a bump the size of a grapefruit, and it was growing fast. In an instant, I had suffered a serious traumatic brain and spinal cord injury that would ultimately impact my life in incredible and unexpected ways.

It was July 3rd, and no one was present in the management office that was just adjacent to the fitness center. I called a friend who worked in a local doctor's office. He advised me to call my primary care doctor, who was also a concussion specialist, which I did. "Do you have the worst headache you've ever had?" No. "Are you nauseous?" I don't think so. "Well, our office is closing early and we are closed tomorrow for July 4th, so if either of those things happen, get yourself to a hospital immediately. We can get you in Saturday morning at 10:00am."

I went back to my place and rested. 'I feel weird, but I'll be ok' I thought. For the next 45 hours, I monitored myself.

I kept the appointment Saturday morning. By that time, my symptoms were indicative of the blow to the head. When I entered the physician's office, I was quite off balance. My eyes were glazed over, my sight was blurred and my speech was off. My doctor could tell I had a serious injury just by looking at me.

At one point, my doctor left the room for a moment. I was experiencing such a bizarre feeling - I was quite aware that I felt so out of it, confused, disoriented. I turned and looked around the room. There was a countertop with some cabinets above. A computer sat on the countertop. There was a chair and exam table. Where am I? I looked back at the door where the doctor had just made her brief exit, and I simply had no idea where I was. I tried to remember. I knew that I had known a moment ago where I was, but suddenly, I didn't remember. It was unsettling.

When the doctor came back in, I told her that I forgot where I was and I guess she must have reminded me. I don't remember much more about my visit, except that they made me do a bunch of 'impact testing'. These tests looked at things like spatial awareness/ interpretation, recall/memory, reaction time and a lot of others that I can't even recall while writing this. One of the tests presented a series of different shapes, and then after a brief pause, showed another series of shapes and asked me to answer yes or no, was this shape the same shape from the first series? What about this shape? This shape? What?! I had no idea. These were really hard! My inability to achieve anywhere close to a successful score - or even finish the tests in the time allotted - was laughable. I was an otherwise very highly functioning professional and individual, but I found these nearly impossible. The results showed cognition of only 0% to 5%. Wow.

That was the beginning of a very new and very different chapter in my life that, believe it or not, has proven to be the best yet. I know what you are probably thinking 'the best yet? That sounds like the worst!', as did a lot of people who constantly reminded me of my halted running career. No longer would I run 13 miles a day; no longer would I even run one mile a day; no longer would I be able to ride a bike.

An athlete my entire life, others found this seemingly devastating. "I can't believe that happened to you! Aren't you mad?!" Mad? Why would I be mad? My friends and colleagues were extremely angry that this 'horrible thing' had happened to me. But in fact, I wasn't angry at all. I didn't define it as a 'horrible thing', only a 'thing' that happened. I just accepted it and moved on. Anger never introduced herself to me.

Maybe I just assumed I would overcome this, too. That's not to say it wouldn't be hard; but I never wasted any anger on it. Now, in retrospect, I see that my friends, family and colleagues instantly recognized the inevitable long and difficult trek ahead but I had no concept of that 'struggle' yet, and therefore, did not attach such a meaning, so on I went, facing each day as it came.

Since I was a young girl, I had been on a path to health and wellness that incorporated good nutrition, physical activity, massage, meditation, acupuncture and overall good physical care. And because of this dedication, I had overcome a variety of health conditions (pancreatitis, hypothyroidism, fibromyalgia, chronic back pain and even a cancer scare) through diet and a healthy lifestyle. Maybe I simply assumed I'd figure out how to gracefully overcome this new situation as well.

That turned out to be a bad assumption; this was going to be different. But with the brain injury, well, I just wasn't thinking clearly.

For weeks I was without phone, sound, light, music, and lay prone much of the time. As my brain began to heal, I started to realize that I was embarking on a very long road to recovery. My traumatic brain injury symptoms were numerous. For months, I spoke with slurred and stuttered speech, suffered short and long-term memory loss, headaches, internal head pressure, blind spots, dizziness, blurred and double vision, vestibular and balance issues, tinnitus, nausea, headaches, pain, impaired depth perception, and just about every symptom associated with such an injury.

From time to time, I forgot where I was, where I lived, and who people were. For example, I might run into someone who looked familiar, but I had no idea if they were a close friend, family member, acquaintance from the gym or the barista at the local Starbucks. The spinal cord injury that resulted from the accident produced unimaginable nerve pain that left me screaming like a suffering wounded animal for hours on end and landed me in the ER on more than one occasion. This injury would ultimately require back surgery: a fusion, laminectomy and removal of a cyst that had formed on my spinal cord. Consequently, I would now have musculoskeletal, neurological and orthopedic issues that would require therapy for years to come - perhaps a lifetime.

I was in banking at the time. Unbeknownst to my employer, when I eventually was able to return to work, I realized that I had literally forgotten how to do parts of my job! For months, I danced a very delicate dance, attempting to slowly relearn the fundamentals of my job, yet at the same time paying very close attention to my brain. If I concentrated too hard or too long, I would get nauseous, dizzy, develop a headache, vision issues and head pressure, basically feeling like I had been re-concussed.

It was extremely difficult navigating through those waters. During my healing, I also learned how stress of any kind - negative emotions, negative people, overexertion etc. - directly and immediately impacted my brain and state of mind, and that became of paramount importance to me.

New to the area in North Carolina and having a career that required working remotely and significant travel, I had not yet established any supportive relationships at the time and therefore, it was going to be entirely up to me to get through this (well, me and my Sheltie-Sheppard-Retriever mix and best companion, Buddy). I continued to hear how angry I 'should be' from friends and colleagues, as if somehow, I should feel a victim.

Something about this injury though, made me firmly declare I would NOT be victim to a simple circumstance of life.

Throughout the healing process, I would be tested. People who offered to help never showed, numerous doctors who maintained my electrical nerve pain was in my head (but it was actually a consequence of the injury - it took persistence on my part and the 10th or 12th doctor finally took images that showed clearly what the problem was), overprescribed medication dosage that left me suicidal, a particularly egocentric doctor who told me that I needed to emotionally accept that I would have serious limitations the rest of my life (I wasn't buying it), a second opinion that urged I needed another fusion and laminectomy STAT (wasn't buyin' that either), and a number of other examples that would infuriate most. But these circumstances only made me dig in further.

I was increasingly determined that no single circumstance, nor the collective would define me as anything other than who I really am at my core. I was not about to become my injury.

I clearly had a choice: to be angry, as most of my friends and colleagues were suggesting, or remain in a positive state of mind. The latter was without question more appealing, as not only was that the best approach to healing my brain and body, but it honestly just seemed more enjoyable. And most importantly, I knew I wasn't a victim and that I would learn something from this experience. But I couldn't seem to break through my baseline. Although I wasn't angry, I did have moments of feeling scared, alone, sad, incredibly confused and highly anxious (these were also symptoms/ consequences of the brain injury). Over time, the anxiety increased significantly, producing profound and intense somatic responses and a couple panic attacks, and I knew I had to do something. I urgently needed to be more committed to my health, especially my brain and my mental health.

I had an epiphany. I began to understand three things very clearly: 1) Whether or not I was conscious of it or not, I was thinking in fear (fear of pain, fear of mounting medical bills, etc.) 2) My thoughts can cause me stress and 3) I can decide what thoughts I want to think.

My world - my reality - literally was transformed when I became committed to my mental hygiene and began to improve my thoughts, attitudes and beliefs. To many, my head injury was an awful tragic event. To me however, it just was what it was. It happened, and I could not change the new circumstances. But I most definitely had the power to change my attitude about the circumstances.

I continued to experiment with improved thinking, speaking, behaving and tried to develop exercises that I could use to refine this ability. I was 150% committed and the more I practiced, the better I felt. And feeling good became my priority so therefore, good thinking was also a priority. The ultimate result was a complete mind redesign. I truly lost my mind and replaced it with a better version! This was LIFE ALTERING!! Through this work, I literally redesigned my mind. This mind redesign has been the greatest, most empowering and profound transformation by far. Eventually, I simply felt a consistent state of bliss and happiness I've never experienced before, and I was - and still am - able to find joy even in the crummiest of situations.

As I was working on writing a book about my mind redesign, my father passed away and my mother's health suffered. Soon after, I was notified that my employment would probably not last more than a few months because of a merger. Shortly following that, a physical injury. It was an extremely trying year and, had these events taken place five years prior, I'm sure I would have been devastated and depressed. But even in my father's passing, I found so much joy and appreciation. In my mother's post-stroke state of being, I found nothing but love and gratitude. Even with my job on the line, I had the inner knowing that all would be well.

Of course, I still have my challenges; certain environments for example, that may trigger the old mind, but I now have the tools to successfully address these challenges. Something happened during the healing process after my injury that altered me forever. I knew that without a doubt, intuitively, but I had no idea about any science that might explain what exactly had altered me and my personality forever.

Throughout my life and corporate career, I have continued to study numerous modalities of healing, a wide variety of approaches to health, and maintained side jobs or hobbies that allowed me to help others (for example, teaching children's yoga, personal training, etc.) One day, about a year after my head injury, I was looking at my five bookshelves. They were filled with books on Ayurveda, herbal remedies, food and mood, acupuncture, applied kinesiology, meditation, breathing, a few different languages (Spanish, Swahili, Italian - languages have always sparked my interest because they allow you to connect with people whom you otherwise could not). The shelves were also lined with books on quantum physics, consciousness, intention, mind-brain-body connection, plant-based nutrition, Zen Buddhism, Qi-Gong, etc.

Then, there was one little bottom shelf on one of the bookcases, where about half the shelf was dedicated to business. Well, that visual told me a LOT! In that moment, I knew what I had to do. Up until that time, I only knew that I wanted to be a better version of me. I knew I wanted to help people. I knew I wanted to connect with people. I knew I wanted to be compassionate.

To that point though I did not know the specifics of what that 'new me' looked like, but suddenly I not only knew and felt in full sensation, what it looked like in my mind and what it felt like in my body. Looking at that bookcase, in an instant I knew what I needed to do, and I made the call that changed everything.

Many of us wait until we are truly suffering to embark on a transformation. In my case, it was a serious, traumatic brain and spinal cord injury. But we do NOT have to wait for an illness, injury or trauma to embark on this amazing journey. We are never too old, too young, too sick, too thin, too fat, too anything. We do not have to wait, and we don't even need a reason to improve our living by improving our thoughts. Why not be happier and more fulfilled, just because?

After the injury, I intuitively developed and implemented tools that allowed me to reconnect with the true and creative essence of myself and create a promising future. I have written a book and a screenplay and am following my bliss and passion. I am by far the happiest I have ever been in my life. I do not worry. I do not believe in lack of anything. Only in abundance. In that moment, looking at the bookcases, I dissolved the past and emerged fully and intentionally into my future. I now live deliberately, with purpose and empowerment.

When you change your outlook on things, look out because things are going to change!

ABOUT THE AUTHOR

 Lynn DelGaudio is an Integrative Health Coach who is passionate about helping organizations and their employees identify negative thoughts and behaviors and designing solutions to help achieve a more positive and productive work culture. After a session with Lynn, you will feel inspired and energized, knowing you are equipped with a plan to move forward in a lasting, positive manner. Lynn loves to help individuals achieve their personal best as they contribute to the welfare of the greater organization. With over 30 years of corporate experience, Lynn works with all levels, from executives, to management teams and in-line employees.

Contact Lynn for coaching and speaking engagements at Lynn@YestoYourHealth.fit.

Learn more at www.yestoyourhealth.fit

I Made a Decision

I was supposed to be a statistic. Black girl, raised by a single mom, on welfare, living in "the 'hood." My fate was to repeat the cycle. What made it worse was that my own father EXPECTED us to follow that cycle. (SMH) My TRUE heavenly Father had a better plan for me!

Praise God!

From a very young age, I have always felt different from my peers. I was never one to follow the crowd, and I was never satisfied with the status quo. My path was different from my family and friends. Most of them are still in my hometown of Buffalo, New York.

I could not WAIT to leave!

Growing up was not easy. My parents divorced, and my mom moved me and my siblings from our beautiful house to a small, cramped apartment. When we first moved in, it was okay. But it swiftly went downhill. It was dangerous. It was rat-infested. There were gangs and drugs. It was all my mom could afford because she was a high school drop-out who never saw herself as a working single mother. She had wanted to be a stay-at-home mom, with a husband and kids to look after. But that was not to be her path.

I had a few brushes with death as a child. I was beaten up several times. The gangs would have "days" where they would terrorize kids going to school. One day was "belt buckle day" where gang members would chase you and try to beat you with a big belt buckle. You quickly learned how to hide if you didn't want to get beaten up. I remember watching from our window as a crowd of gang members following the leader with a gun swarmed into our apartment complex looking for a fight.

But I always knew this wasn't the life for me. I made a decision every day that I would not continue to live like this. I didn't want to associate with rough kids. I saw so many of the neighborhood kids get hooked on smoking and drinking and drugs. So many of them gave up hope. Several of my relatives smoked and drank. Every time I saw them, or smelled their breath, I said to myself, "I will not live like them."

Once on a public bus, an adult man tried to fondle me, and I yelled and kicked him as hard as I could and pushed him off the seat into the aisle. You picked the wrong girl to mess with, buddy. No one stepped up to help me. No one berated him. I moved to another seat and everyone just went about their own business. That was just a normal day for me as I grew up.

At age 12, I contemplated committing suicide. It was the lowest point in my life. I was sick of being afraid all the time. I was tired of never having things. I looked around and saw no hope. But my grandmother Evelyn talked me out of it. She took the time to show me how to talk to God as a Father and a friend. She taught me how to turn to Him and rely on His strength. Since that time, He has always guided my life.

I realized that my earthly father was incapable of getting us out of our situation. He was okay with us living on welfare so long as he had money for him to smoke and drink and hang out with his friends. It wasn't that he didn't love us, it's just that he did not expect better for his life or ours.

But I certainly did.

I worked hard to get good grades in school and that determination paid off when I was offered a chance to attend a private all-girls high school. The school was in the suburbs. To get there involved two different city buses and about three hours of travel each way. Out of 400 girls, there were only three of us black girls. One of the other girl couldn't put up with the derogatory comments and disrespect and dropped out after our freshmen year. Then there was just 2 of us who graduated from there.

I have a knack for getting along with everyone. I did my thing, stayed out of trouble, kept my head down and worked hard. I even inspired my mom to get her GED and to start college. One of the best memories in my life is in May 1976 when I graduated from high school, my little sister graduated from 8th grade, and my mom graduated from college. It was a special time.

I never planned to attend college. I wanted to enter the military, but after my mom's positive experience in college, she talked me into attending. During my freshman year, guys were asking me out. One guy was especially interested and persistent. He was a junior from New York City. I didn't make it easy for him, I will admit, because I knew I could not marry anyone who had even the slightest inclination that it was okay to live on welfare. As I got to know him, I learned that he spoke two languages, he was a pre-med with aspirations of being a family practice physician.

We began dating and eventually married between his second and 3rd year of medical school. We have been married for 39 years and have raised three wonderful boys who have never had to spend a single day afraid in their lives. They have not wanted for anything. They got the best education, we live in a wonderful home in a wonderful community. All because I made a decision to not repeat the cycle of poverty.

I have become a successful mom and entrepreneur through wanting better, learning to do better, making better choices, and walking with my God.

The fabric of my life has been woven by the master weaver My Father God! As I have matured, and as life continues to throw me curve balls, I cannot impress upon you how I cherish that relationship to this day. The closer we become, the more I trust Him to lead me and guide me. When I follow His lead, I NEVER go wrong. I am constantly and acutely aware of His loving guiding hand.

With that said, yes, God will guide you, but YOU still have a part to play. Here are three steps I recommend anyone take to better their lives:

1. First, get a hotel for a weekend or find a retreat weekend somewhere. NO TV, PHONE, RADIO,

INTERNET, etc. Spend that whole weekend talking to God. Ask Him "What is YOUR plan for my life?" Pay attention to what you feel and hear. Make notes and write down everything that comes up. You'll discover some important nuggets of wisdom, I promise.

2. Second, DECIDE to do what He tells you. You will have to read books, take courses, find mentors, etc. to make it happen. You will have to make changes in your life, but they will all be worth it.

3. CHOOSE your path and be alert to things that come your way that will help you on your way. Always remember: "for your life to change, YOU have to change." Doing the same thing over and over and expecting different results is the definition of insanity.

ABOUT THE AUTHOR

Robin Nazon has been a successful entrepreneur for the past 40 years. She loves empowering people with the resources and tools they can use to live a more successful life. She helps businesses grow and prosper.

Her first experience with entrepreneurship was watching her grandmother and friends cook and sell chicken dinners from her kitchen. Although she was only four years old at the time, she already liked the idea of working for herself and doing what she enjoyed.

Her first adult foray into entrepreneurship was Amway, then Worldcom, then The People's Network. Her entire team at The People's Network joined PrePaid Legal, which then became Legal Shield. She once heard it said that people generally need to try seven different opportunities before they find a home. She lucked out and found it with company #5. She has been empowering people with access to legal assistance to protect their rights for the last 20 years and will continue to forever work toward making Martin Luther King's dream of equal justice a reality.

She has taught CPR classes for over 30 years, making her a true lifesaver.

She graduated in 1982 from S.U.N.Y Binghamton, NY with a BA in Psychology. She is happily married for 39 years to her husband Herold. She is the mother of three fabulous sons, Alex, Malcolm and Eric.

She loves God.

She loves life.

She loves helping people.

To learn more about Legal Shield, visit https://rnazon.ladiesofjustice.com

To contact Robin for speaking engagements email RobinNazon@gmail.com

Overcoming Obstacles Made Me a Stronger Person

Life is full of opposition and obstacles. It may not feel like it at the time, but obstacles are important.

Obstacles help us become the person God created us to be. In my life, I have experienced numerous challenges I thought would destroy me. But they ended up making me a better person.

At age 5, I was placed in foster care and became a ward of the state of Maryland. I was taken away from everything I knew. I was taken away from my family and friends. I was in the home of total strangers with no warning or preparation and I didn't know anything.

Being put in foster care meant that I was removed from an unhealthy, unstable environment and put into a healthier, stable environment. I was removed from an environment where my two older brothers would steal food in order for us to eat to an environment where I ate three meals a day. Although the new environment was more conducive for me mentally, emotionally, physically and spiritually, at 5-years-old I didn't grasp the concept.

I was trying to understand what took place. I was scared. I was afraid. I didn't want to be in foster care. I wanted my mother. I wanted to go back home. I knew how to function and survive in the old environment. But the new place was totally different. I didn't know how to function or survive in the new environment.

Questions bombarded my mind. They came so fast I couldn't speak the questions in order to get an answer. Where am I? Why am I here? How long will I be here? When will I go back home? Who are these people? Why are they looking at me? Where is my mom? When will she come and get me? So many questions; all left unanswered. I was in a whirlwind and didn't know how to get out!

Every day I had to adjust to being in foster care. When I thought I had things figured out, I was thrown a curve ball. I had to establish a relationship with my new family. I didn't know what to call them. I asked if I could call them mom and dad. I was told that if that's what I wanted to call them, it was alright with them. So, I began calling them mom and dad. Then, one day, my biological mother came to visit me. I was completely surprised and confused. I didn't know what to call her. I was so uncomfortable. It got to the point that I never called my foster mother "mom" when my biological mother was around. I didn't understand the concept of having two mothers; one who is in your life providing and taking care of you, and the other who visits occasionally.

I also had to learn how to overcome the broken promises of my biological mother. In my heart, when she would tell me she would be back to see me, I was excited. I expected her to come in a timely manner. I anticipated her visits but felt great hurt and disappointment when she didn't return as promised. My foster mom would explain that maybe she didn't have transportation or that something happened beyond her control. In other words, she meant well but she couldn't keep the promise. My foster mom would do something special for me when my mother didn't keep her promises. Sometimes she would buy me something and other times we just spend time together.

I made a vow to myself that when I became a mom, I would never make promises to my children. And I never did. I always told them, "If I could."

In foster care, I really blossomed. As I reached my teen years, I began to understand that my situation was completely different from my friends and peers. I was accepted by some of my friends who knew my situation but there were others who treated me like I was an outsider. Like I didn't belong. Like they were better than me because they lived with their parents. What they didn't realize is that I wanted what they had. But, later in life I also realized they wanted what I had. The love of parents and a home. I realized they had their parents and a house but not the love and a home.

As I grew into a teenager, things changed. When I first went into foster care I had an African American social worker by the name of Mrs. Bailey. She was my social worker for years. She transported me back and forth to medical appointments and I grew to know her as a person. I felt comfortable with her. One day out of the blue, I was introduced to a new social worker by the name of Mrs. Waters. She was a Caucasian social worker and right away I felt uncomfortable. I no longer had someone who looked like me and I could identify with. Don't get me wrong, Mrs. Waters was a very nice lady. However, she didn't look like me.

I was born in the 60's and grew up in the 70's. I was in an all-black school until third grade when I was integrated into the white school. So, imagine the time frame I was living and having a Caucasian social worker picking me up from school and taking me to my medical appointments! Can you imagine the looks we received? Can you imagine the shock on everyone's faces? Can you even fathom the questions that were running through their minds? Better yet, can you imagine the looks that said, "I know you're in foster care? My money is being spent on taking care of you." Can you imagine how I felt as a teenager? I wanted to find a hole and crawl in it! I wanted to be invisible!

I remember when Mrs. Waters took me to my eye appointment and I was looking at the different frames. I saw a pair I really liked. However, the lady who waited on me took me to another section and told me these were the glasses covered by Medicaid. I was so embarrassed. Everyone sitting in the waiting area heard her. I wanted to die on the spot. Once again, my foster mom explained to me that yes, I did have Medicaid, but it didn't change who I was as a person. I was still someone special and Jesus loved me despite what people may think about me.

My foster mom believed in education. She held me to a higher standard when it came to education. She selected all my classes while I was in high school. The classes were the highest levels you could take and she would tell me the grades she expected me to obtain in the classes; mainly A's and B's. I didn't like or agree with some of her selections, but I took the classes. The classes were hard and there were times when I struggled. I didn't bring home A's and B's all the time; I had some C's as well. If she knew that I did my best, she was content with the C's.

I didn't understand then that my foster mother saw my potential. I didn't realize at the time that she was preparing me for college. For as long as I could remember I wanted to go to college. My foster mother ensured that my dream would be fulfilled if I put the work in. I was inducted into the National Honor Society (NHS) my sophomore year in high school and maintained the standard of remaining in the NHS until I graduated.

Although I was a member of the NHS, my school counselor told me that I wasn't college material. My foster mother, on the other hand, told me that I was.

I took steps to research everything I needed to apply and get accepted to colleges. I learned the dates, signed up for my SATs and took the tests. I had my high school transcripts and SATs sent to different colleges and my foster mom provided for me financially. I had worked during the summer and she instructed me to open a bank account and save money for college. The money I saved assisted me in purchasing clothes, suitcases and other items for college.

We were preparing for college before I was accepted. I received acceptance letters from Salisbury State University, University of Maryland Baltimore County and Delaware State College (DSC) now known as Delaware State University (DSU). We had a decision to make.

While going through this process, my former social worker, Mrs. Baily, was reinstated as my social worker. She came to the house and mom informed her that I had been accepted to three colleges. When she heard that I had been accepted by DSC, she informed me that her ex-brother-in-law worked at DSC. She called him and based upon her word, he took me into his home and treated me as part of his family. His name was Nelson Townsend. He was the Athletic Director for DSC. I lived with his family until he was able to obtain a room for me on campus. He also assisted me in getting a work study job with the Office of Student Accounts. I used the money I earned to pay my school tuition.

I was the first person from my family to attend college. I graduated with a Bachelor of Science degree in Community Health and owed the college nothing. I was debt free. I have worked with the State of Delaware for 30 years. What my school counselor said was impossible became possible when I was accepted and graduated from DSC.

How did I overcome my obstacles? How did I survive? I learned to accept the process God had ordained for my life. It wasn't a process I would have chosen, but God knew what was best for me. I survived because I learned how to adapt and work the process. A process is defined by the English Oxford Living Dictionary as "a series of actions or steps taken in order to achieve a particular end."

While in foster care, I took the necessary steps to adapt to the changes that took place in my life. Instead of being mad and angry, I took advantage of the situation presented to become a better person. I accepted the caring, loving, and nurturing environment I was placed in. I accepted the fact that I was not returning home to my biological mother. I accepted the fact that my biological mother did the best she could, but that God had a better plan for my life. I excelled because my foster mother pushed me into purpose.

The greatest and most important reason I survived was because of God! Everything that took place in my life was orchestrated and ordained by Him. He became my Lord and Savior at an early age, and He guided me through some very difficult situations in my life. My foster parents were the vessels He used to ensure that I reached the "expected end" He had for my life.

I developed a relationship with my foster parents that exceeded way beyond my aging out of foster care. They continued to pour into my life when, according to the state of Maryland, it was no longer necessary. They were and still remain my mom and dad. They both have gone home to be with the Lord, but I still have the memories and the wisdom they imparted into my life.

No matter what obstacle you may encounter in life, remember that you can overcome it. I would like to encourage every child who is in foster care that God has a plan for your life. God hasn't abandoned you. He loves you and always wants the best for you. You can survive and thrive in foster care. Your obstacles will make you a better person.

ABOUT THE AUTHOR

Mary Johnson earned a Bachelor of Science degree in Community Health and began her state career at her alma mater, Delaware State University. She worked at her alma mater for two and a half years in the capacity of a microfilm photographer/ typist and later was employed by the Division of Public Health as a Public Health Educator with the Adolescent Health Program. Mary works in the capacity of a Trainer/Educator III and serves diverse communities in Sussex County by setting up programs that encompasses a wide variety of health issues.

Mary enjoys acting, theater, reading, writing, sports, and spending time with her family. She is an ordained minister and serves in various positions at Pilgrims Ministry of Deliverance.

Mary is the mother of two adult children, Jessica and Keith.

Her life validates her motto, "Just because you are down, doesn't mean you're out!"

To contact Mary for speaking engagements, email her at Marycatjohn54@outlook.com.

How I "Exposed" Myself to

My Destiny

I have always been a creative person. I have an intense and unique personality and a mind that never sleeps even when it sleeps. But despite my artistic skills and creative tendencies, I never truly found my niche until I moved to Alaska in January of 2000 and began playing with a camera for more than snapshots. Truly, you cannot live in that state and not embrace the beauty in some form. I took many nature photos and submitted five to the Alaska state fair amateur photo competition where I received a blue ribbon and two honorable mentions. A friend at the time said, "I think you've found your niche."

A few years later, I took some photography classes from the basics of photography to "finding your niche." At that point I truly believed I would specialize in adolescent teens as I had already brought the personalities out of several socially awkward and timid seniors and middle schoolers.

My divorce in 2009 led me to feel as though I was damaged goods. I was overweight, barely educated, pushing 50 and felt I had nothing to offer a member of the opposite sex or the world.

It was during a pity party conversation with a friend that I confessed what I'd kept telling myself, "Who would want 'this'?" I told him. He proceeded to tell me I was beautiful, smart, funny, talented and simply needed to get my "sexy back." Then, everything fell into place when he spoke those eight simple words... "Be beautiful and let the world catch up." After his pep talk and kind words, motivated, I went into the bathroom and stripped down. I strategically put my cell phone on selfie mode, covered my breasts with my adjoining arm, made a sexy pose and took the shot. Cropping it, I posted it as my profile photo on social media and the positive responses were just what I needed to boost my confidence and ensure me maybe my friend was right.

So, I began being my own model, posing and 'getting my sexy back' through various images. I made a secret online gallery of the images and several months later showed them to some female colleagues. "I'm thinking of starting a business doing 'oohh-la-la' shots," I told them. "But I want to specialize in women over 40 and chunky chicks. Women who may feel they don't have it anymore. I want to show them they ARE beautiful." The ladies loved the images of me and volunteered to be my next models in assisting me build my portfolio, promotional materials and begin my business.

I chose the name Focus on Fabulous because that is exactly what I did. I focused on what was fabulous, beautiful, lovely and extraordinary about my subjects. A woman's image of herself is something most men don't understand. Women, no matter their age, shape or size, will find some flaw with their body. I decided to capture the beauty that resides within each client and transform their confidence and self-esteem by bringing the inside to the outside. I have since been dubbed a "transformation artist" by my clients.

The road was slow, and the clients were scarce, but I had truly found my niche and loved what I was I doing. The ladies bragged about their photos and had me reveal them to guests at a party we attended. This is where I met the man who eventually would become my husband and business advocate.

It was a brisk February day when I arrived in Charleston, South Carolina with my boyfriend and his thirteen-year-old son. We relocated from the Florida panhandle so he could take a job with a global company based out of that city. My boyfriend hit the ground running and within a week was traveling out of state which made the transition even more hectic as we needed to get my stepson enrolled in school, find a place to live and establish residency.

Once our lives settled, routines were created, and the house made to be a home, the need for me to seek gratification outside those walls arose often. Having been a Certified Nursing Assistant in Florida, I had planned to transfer my qualifications to my new state, but the State of South Carolina would not accept my credentials. Plus, my stepson was having difficulty dealing with the transition. This presented an obstacle in seeking outside employment because I felt my primary role was to be there for him.

By being a nursing assistant, I was previously able to work in home health care which provided the flexibility I desired. With that option no longer available to me, I thought to myself, "So, now what?" It was in a conversation with my boyfriend that he said, "Why don't you do something with your photography? You're an award-winning photographer and you're in a beautiful place." And that is precisely what I did.

By December 2012 I was promoting Focus on Fabulous Creative Photography full force with an emphasis on boudoir-type photography.

I attended every networking event, meeting, and small business group I could find, often six to seven a week promoting my services. It was during one of those meetings I met a new business owner whose mission was to help small business women, learn, connect, grow and prosper in their businesses. It was during a one-on-one meeting with her that I discovered I was unknowingly targeting the wrong audience.

I was convinced that my ideal client was women who were over 40 and perhaps felt like they didn't have what it took to portray sexy any longer. To my surprise, after the questions and data were tallied, I was shocked to see that my main audience was women of confidence who enjoyed feeling sexy and beautiful, not the woman with low self-esteem. In fact, my ideal client was the hard-working, attractive, woman who enjoyed being in the spotlight and doing things for herself to continually make herself feel more attractive and confident.

With this new information in my toolbox I set forth with gusto promoting my business. As one of only a few boudoir photographers in the area, my pricing was competitive, my approach unique and my talent as good, if not better than what was out there. I was confident in my ability to succeed. However, despite my availability through website, freelance sites, and my continuous give-a-ways, promotions and special occasion package rates for holidays like Mother's Day and Christmas, I was not acquiring the leads and ultimately receiving the business I needed. I ultimately chose to make this niche a hobby rather than a business.

It was during that time that a message appeared on a freelance site from a young lady in Ohio. Her fiancé was stationed here in the Navy and she was entering the Navy within the next two months. She wanted an "oohh-la-la" book for him to have while she was at bootcamp when they would have no contact and asked if I could squeeze a shoot in during the weekend that she would be in the area visiting him. Of course, I obliged.

She and her fiancé showed up for the shoot and we had an amazing time. He was overjoyed with the images that he merely saw through the lens of my camera. As the shoot was winding down, I asked for a special photo that I had envisioned. It only used her crossed legs sporting a cute pair of red slides and his dog tags. She agreed, and the image was captured. Her fiancé and I exchanged information as to when we could meet and give him the book once it was completed as she would be in boot camp and inaccessible.

As I edited her images for her book, I also edited the image I requested. The image moved me. It had an old Americana "pin up" style to it and was unique. I thought to myself, "This would make a great magazine cover." I have had numerous images featured in magazines and was considering submitting this image to a few when the thought crossed my mind. "I have been writing since I could pick up a pencil, I've been a graphic designer for over 20 years, I'm already a photographer. I should just start my own magazine."

I posted the image on my personal social media with the caption, I think I'm going to start a magazine that focuses on the hidden unseen beauty in our world.

Many people commented that they would like to be a part of that, write for it, read it and so forth.

That was mid-June and September 8, 2015 Focus on Fabulous magazine was launched. A measly 20-page publication featuring content about everyday women living extraordinary lives yet proudly featuring amazing women like a 23-year-old young lady working to build houses and a rehabilitation community for homeless veterans, and another woman whose sole mission in life is empowering confidence in young underprivileged girls. As of this writing we have completed over three years and 14 issues and are available in both digital and print formats.

People ask me all the time, "How did you get into starting a magazine?" and I truly answer, "It was a whim. I just took the leap." I asked myself, "How hard can it be?" I had no training and little pertinent experience, but I had basic overall knowledge and I had tenacity.

In researching about publishing magazines, I discovered a program I did not know. I had to learn it and am still learning. I discovered about distribution, postage, where to find content when you come up short and so forth. I set up an advisory board of business professionals whose expertise and opinions I admired to assist in my endeavors and explained that I was truly "winging" it. We tossed around ideas like digital or print and why. Paid publication or free and how to solicit advertisers when you're just getting started.

It has been a roller coaster ride and I fire myself at least once a month, ready to give up. But then something happens to remind me that this is my mission, my calling, my destiny. My ministry. The mark I will leave on this world.

I am reminded that I am Michelle Bryant Griffin, owner and CEO or Focus on Fabulous, LLC, a digital and print media company that shines light and beauty on what might otherwise go unnoticed or be overlooked. I have been dubbed a transformation artist by my clients, colleagues and peers because I reveal the silver lining, the lovely and fabulous in any situation or individual.

I am one of a long line of creative intellects and givers with huge hearts. We proudly speak our minds, standing tall, showing the world the value and beauty of the overlooked, misunderstood or underappreciated. We give hope to the hopeless, motivation to the hopeful and encouragement to the everyday individual. As a photographer by instinct, artist by birthright, writer, poet and free spirit, truth, unbridled love and transparency are the cornerstone in which I build my business, message, and how I shall leave my mark.

I build. I set free, expose...myself and others. I reveal the unseen beauty. Bringing the light to the outside, I liberate, loosen and challenge others to step out of their comfort zones and awaken themselves to the possibilities of what lies within thus shining light to the world. I blend story and heart, passion and purpose together to expose the masterpiece of each I encounter. It is through this business that hand in hand I toot the horn of the shy, the oppressed or forgotten, shines light on the strength behind the scars. And although I view the world through lenses of pink, I bark at the breeze, creating a thunder of determination in rooting for the underdog because it is a journey I know well and a path in which unites us.

I shall change the world one relationship at a time, one story at a time because through my own transformation I share my moments, my flaws and my light with a transparent and passionate purpose that all shall feel worthy, wanted and revered. This I will do even beyond my final breath.

I literally have the best job in the world. I GET to meet amazing women. I get to toot their horns and liberate them, to hear their stories, share their obstacles and tell the world about the challenges they have overcome. Everyone has a story. Your story matters and can change someone's life. That's why I'm telling this story for this book.

It is my desire that as you read this story you do not let obstacles get you down or stop you from using your talents, that you look outside the box at other ways to share your passion with the world. Had I not found my mentor, who looked at my business from the outside, who knows where I might have ended.

Find someone you trust to be honest about your strengths, weaknesses, talents and flaws. Learn to accept the challenges and the assistance from others who offer areas where you may be weak. Just jump. Take the leap. And do not worry about failing.

When I compare my current issue to my first issue, I smile. I was so proud of myself for getting that first issue done. Since it was my first, I was learning everything about putting a magazine together, including the software. The imperfections and lack of expertise are blatant. But now, 14 issues later, I proudly show it to anyone because from that first issue to the latest one, you can see where I came from, the growth, the talent, professionalism, the strength, and the tenacity.

I am proud to say I have touched lives, told the stories of the underdog, showcased the hard-working and celebrated the silver lining in everything and circumstance. In fact, ironically my publication focuses on the hard-working, attractive woman who enjoys being in the spotlight and doing things for herself and others but often prefers to remain in the shadows. By featuring them in this way I get to continually make her feel more attractive and confident in a whole different way. At Focus on Fabulous magazine, page after page, issue after issue you will discover that we motivate, educate, celebrate and encourage our audience. We are not just a magazine. We are an experience.

ABOUT THE AUTHOR

 Michelle Bryant is multi-talented. Growing up the oldest of eight children, she was destined to be a leader, mentor, and motivator. As an entrepreneur, artist, speaker, self-published author of five books, and a multi-award winning, published photographer, she has shared her story, passion, and

light thorough various engagements such as a Colorado Springs Mothers of Prayer group and a group of domestic violence victims in Jacksonville, Florida.

She has appeared on the nationally syndicated radio broadcast "The Healing Touch with Norma Dearing" and KTLF 90.5 in Colorado Springs and on Charleston's local radio show "It's Your Business." In addition, Michelle has ministered to over two dozen youth at a residential treatment facility for boys and girls under the age of eighteen, suffering from emotional issues such as abuse and neglect. Michelle assisted the Georgia Public School Board with Special Needs elementary school children, and while she held her Florida Certified Nursing Assistance license worked one on one with brain injured and Dementia clients.

She attended 27 schools in twelve years, has lived in or traveled to all 50 states including Alaska, Hawaii and Puerto Rico and driven across Canada three times and been to Mexico and the Bahamas. Michelle also served as an Air Force wife for over twenty years. Her time spent at Ringling School of Art and Design, proved to be the catapult to her creativity and has provided education, insight, and lessons she carries with her to this day.

She shines her light and speaks from her heart in an encouraging, inspiring and transparent manner about her childhood and adolescence of abuse, a struggling marriage and the trials, tribulations and emotional damages occurred; yet offers a message of victory and empowerment, healing and hope, to those who feel they are alone in their own personal wars.

To book Michelle for a powerful and encouraging speaking engagement email her at mnawethr@gmail.com.

To submit a story, subscribe or contribute content or for information on Focus on Fabulous magazine visit her website at www.fofmagazine.com.

Her books can be found at most online retailers or her amazon page https://www.amazon.com/c.-michelle-bryant/e/B00KQ2OSM8.

For her photography and general information: www.divinelyfocused.com

I Skipped Town to Save My Sanity

It was a good day. The sun was shining, the birds were chirping. It was the last day of school for my children. And it was the last day of my sanity. It was the day my very possessive boyfriend decided to attack me.

While getting ready to go with him to his son's graduation, I received a message from a friend who needed me. I've learned that when we take time to help a friend by listening, you just may be able to save their life. So that is what I did, I listened. While trying to be there for my friend, I heard a loud boom where my door burst open. It was him.

"Who are you on the phone with?" he demanded. I told him that he wouldn't know. At that point, no more words were spoken, just the feeling of a fist striking my face. Quick to react, I swung back, and we started to fight. I could hear my children screaming, "Get off of my mommy!" Because of this, I immediately stopped and quickly reminded him with an intent to diffuse the situation that he was going to his own son's graduation. Instead of stopping, he replied, "I'm going to hell or jail." I immediately felt, due to past experiences, that he might try to kill me.

My attacker turned and walked out of the door and began to damage my car so that I wouldn't be able to get away from him. He flattened my tires, broke my windows, and popped the hood of the car to start beating the motor and battery. While these things were happening, I began to fear for my life. I called the cops who unfortunately didn't show up until several hours later.

He began to throw rocks at my house which resulted in me having busted windows. He poured gas around my home while my children and I were still in there. My attacker was truly a mad man. I ran out of the house in hopes that he wouldn't light it on fire.

Instead, while standing outside with no protection from a man whom I once loved and trusted, he began to throw rocks at me. I didn't know what was on his mind. I was yelling and screaming for him to please stop and pleading for my kids' safety. but nothing worked.

My cries fell on deaf ears. He ran up on the porch where I was standing and tried to hit me with a brick, but I began to kick at him. Suddenly, my eight-year-old daughter ran out of the house with a knife and began to yell, "Leave my mommy alone!" That was truly an awakening for me. I took the knife from my baby and began chasing him! I knew at that moment I had to protect my children by any means necessary.

My attacker ran from me and didn't come back for several hours. I found out later that he ran into a family member of mine who was walking with his wife and his own children. My attacker ran up to him and started beating him with a bat yelling, "If I can't get her, I'll get whoever is the closest to her."

I was heart-broken to learn that my cousin was in the hospital with a broken arm. I knew that something must be done.

I walked to the police department, filed a complaint, and got a restraining order. To my surprise, my attacker was following me. He was hiding in the bushes calling my phone while I was at the police department threatening to kill me. I had to act fast. I immediately got my kids out of the house afraid that he might come back that night and finish what he started earlier that day by trying to set the house on fire.

After my children were gone, I stayed in the house alone with the lights off so he couldn't see through the window that he had previously busted. Because we lived in the city, there were bars on the windows. Thank God because that's what kept him out. To my surprise he was outside just as I suspected pouring gasoline around my house again! This time, while he was in the back I immediately ran out the front. This was a nightmare that I couldn't seem to wake up from.

The next day, I traded my car in and got a new one. I rented a U-Haul, put my stuff in storage, and I skipped town.

I left my family along with everything that I knew to be home. I left with one television, my kids, my car, and a week's worth of clothing for all of us. We fled to South Carolina which is now where I currently reside. I left an unhealthy and abusive relationship with no job in sight and far away from the life that I once knew. I had to quit my job in New Jersey due to this domestic abuse. I was on unemployment.

When I got to South Carolina, I had to apply for public assistance but due to the unemployment, no assistance was granted. I tried living off my unemployment paying one thousand dollars in rent plus all utilities. My unemployment was about eight hundred dollars every two weeks which wasn't enough.

I did what I had to do to pick up the pieces. While my children where in school, I was consistently out looking for work. It wasn't easy. I was in this new place where I didn't know anybody. I sometimes got lost not even knowing how to get back home.

Then it hit me. I know how to drive, so why not try a cab company. I looked in the yellow pages and called a company. I was immediately hired. I was so excited! I was now away from this mad man, and for my family things had started to look up. I was making over $100 a day. Everything seemed to be going well until I found out that my attacker moved to South Carolina to find me. Immediately my heart sank. ((WHAT HAPPENED?))

The moral of my story is: if I could drop everything, leave my job, and my family, and come to an unfamiliar place to be free and get out of an abusive relationship, you can too! I encourage you to get out now! That is my advice to anyone in an abusive situation. You can end up dead.

When I think of the title of this book, I am inspired as I think of all I had to endure to get to where I am today. I now own a small trucking company; ACM trucking and logistics because I know if I can't do anything else, I can drive. I have an online adult novelty store as well as a credit repair company. All three of my companies are a direct result of the trials that I had to endure.

For instance, I couldn't get a mortgage, so I started repairing my credit. Because of that, I now offer credit repair services at a reduced rate to prevent homelessness due to poor credit scores. I hope and pray that my story can inspire and enlighten someone in an abusive relationship to GET OUT! You are beautiful, you are valued, and your life is worth way more than any person who is physically, mentally, emotionally, sexually, financially and monetarily abusing you. Abuse comes in all different forms.

Please know the signs. Don't ignore the red flags. Sometimes we see the signs, but we tend to ignore them because we can be so caught up in the way a person makes us feel. It's okay for you to love yourself. It's okay for you to value yourself. It's okay to walk with your head held high knowing you overcame the obstacles that were put in your path.

I want to leave every person male or female with this thought, you can overcome the abuse. Yes, it will hurt. Take your time to heal because healing can be draining. Healing is just like fighting another battle, however, this battle is one that is worth fighting for. Look in the mirror and tell yourself I am beautiful, I am special, and I am worth more than to be somebody's punching bag. Hurt people hurt people. Always keep your head up and don't forget to love yourself unconditionally.

ABOUT THE AUTHOR

 Christina Mullins is an entrepreneur. She owns four businesses including Royal Credit Services, Royal Getaways, ACM Transportation and Logistics, and Mrz Peachez Pleasurez.

She also controls one non-profit organization, Royal Beauties Inc., whose mission is to responsibly service our troubled teens and single parents in an informative manner. Her goal is to reach and teach and provide clients with the appropriate tools that will equip them for a more productive life.

Her life experiences have taught her that the most important thing in life is love, appreciation and giving back.

She is the mother of four and Grandmother of one. She wears many hats in life.

To contact her about her businesses or to invite her to speak to your church or youth group, call 1(800)322-4819 or email acmullins@royalcreditservices.com or visit websites Royalcreditservices.com

Royalgetaways.inteletravel.com

Mrzpeachezpleasurez.com

I Became an Optimist

I was born on an August Saturday in 1979, the fourth child to a married (not sure happily) and very overwhelmed twenty-three-year-old woman. I don't know much about her in this stage of her life. I did come to learn later in life that she had lost her mother very early to heart disease. I learned that the 23-year-old woman went on to have a very successful career in the US Army and upon retiring became employed by the Department of Veterans Affairs and has been honored by the legislature of her state.

However, on that August Saturday in 1979 she made what I believe to be one of the most difficult sacrifices of her life. She made the decision to give me up to become a ward of the state of South Carolina. I have often tried to place myself in her mindset. It plays out several different ways. As I mature, as I become more of who I am to be, each version changes. The latest version is proud that I came from the womb of a dynamic and complex woman. For at least three days or better I remained nameless. I promise that this is not a sad story. It is a depiction of my journey from unworthiness and low self-esteem to optimism.

I, the nameless baby, would end up in the arms of a widowed mother of three girls. Although she and a man she would eventually marry adopted me three years later and provided me with more adoration than should probably be allowed, I still carried a set of burdens. Burdens which seemed to be of an unknown origin. For the longest of time, I felt this insatiable need to "earn my keep." I often felt out of place even though no one in my immediate family did anything to warrant me feeling this way. It was kind of odd that I was given the last name of my Mama's first husband who died before I was born. It made for a longer than necessary explanation when people inquired.

I was the darkest of my Mama's children and very tall. People often questioned the origin of my height and my Mama would retort by saying that she had tall people in her family. I wasn't quite sure if people were to know that I was adopted or if it was a secret. In fact, I learned that I was adopted through the taunting of one of my older cousins.

I went to school in the early eighties and nineties, before this abundance of melanin in my skin was celebrated or even acknowledged as beautiful. Not to mention that I was chubbier than most. At the age of ten I was at least 5 feet 6 inches tall, weighed about 150 pounds, wore a size 10 shoe and sported a Jheri curl. Although I was very smart, my classmates reminded me that I was fat, black and ugly at least once a week. They even thought it was hilarious to call me sow – a female pig. Elementary and middle school proved to be a great breeding ground for my insecurities.

I negotiated an acceptable rhythm and navigated high school pretty well and graduated as the Valedictorian of my class. I couldn't wait to leave my hometown and excel at the College of Charleston. It was there that my skin color was celebrated but my race also warranted the questioning of my worthiness or my belonging on the campus. There were many who thought that I did not earn my spot at the college but was gifted the spot through affirmative action. Imagine that – I went from being the one everyone thought would always have the right answer to being questionable. College wasn't all bad and I got through it and graduated in the four years my parents had allotted.

Now off to the job market. I remember the year 2001 and the number I put down as my desired salary on every job application - $30,000. I thought I was low balling, but I had to start somewhere. Then I remember the day the interviewer laughed so hard and told me that I would need to leave South Carolina if I thought that I would make $30,000 right out of college. Sometimes I think I should have heeded her advice. Nonetheless, I stayed and accepted mediocre salaries believing if I just got my foot in the door, I could prove my worth – once again "earn my keep." I replayed that song and dance for several years and change of careers.

It wasn't until I found myself working with a group of young girls at my church that I felt like I had finally found something that agreed with my spirit and it almost didn't matter what the salary was. Life was great until there was a change in our executive branch. With the new administration came new priorities which unfortunately did not include the funding source for my beloved job. I persisted working without pay (but with a promise to pay) for six months. It was during that time that led to one of the most stressful times in my life.

The funny thing about stress is most of the time you don't feel like you even have time to acknowledge it. I can now remember the multiple occasions I felt my heart skip beats and then race to catch up. I can now remember the ever so slight tightening of my chest. I can now remember my breath being taken away. I can now remember the cold sweats and exhaustion. However, then, it wasn't until I heard the doctor utter the words "there's no need to do a stress test, it's evident you've had a heart attack." I was a thirty-one-year-old wife and mother to two young children. I told the doctor that clearly, he was wrong and that I didn't even have time to have a heart attack.

Allow me to reintroduce myself, I am Keisha Hawes and I survived a heart attack. Now that I have your attention, you must make me this promise. I want you to pause at this moment and read this aloud.

If she can have a heart attack at the age of 31, then I will learn my risk factors and adjust my lifestyle accordingly. Heart disease is the number 1 killer of women in America, killing more women than all forms of cancer combined. The thought of heart disease was nowhere on my radar at the time of my heart attack. I then had a choice to make and I had to make it quickly. I was at a crossroads. I had started down the path of self-pity, anger and blame (everyone other than myself). The choice I needed to make was to decide how I wanted to frame what had happened to me. I could remain stagnant, believing that I had suffered a heart attack, or I could move forward in gratitude believing that I had survived a heart attack. It was in developing an attitude of gratitude that I also adopted a lifestyle of optimism.

By putting this lifestyle of optimism into action, I was able to move from Keisha Hawes the 31-year-old heart attack to Keisha Hawes the national spokesperson for the Go Red for Women campaign of the American Heart Association. I am passionate about advocacy for women and youth. I am a survivor of circumstances that could have caused my life to go in many different directions. I believe that when properly equipped we can overcome anything. My goal is to use my voice and resources to empower women and youth to use their pitfall experiences as a platform to empower others, to find purpose in their pain.

Developing a lifestyle of optimism does not mean that your life will be exempt of challenges. Living optimistically means that you know that the challenge is not your destination. It is a part of your journey. A challenge is sent to teach. Once you learn, your next task is to share what you've learned to help someone else. Foster care and adoption taught me how to receive love and lend a helping hand. Being bullied taught me how to be a good friend and embrace my uniqueness. Losing taught me how to win gracefully. Lacking taught me to share. Surviving a heart attack taught me how to eat healthier, exercise and ask for help. My heart attack at 31 in truth saved my life. Because of having this challenge as early as I did my heart sustained minimal damage and recovery was easier.

Everyday life will present you with opportunities and challenges. Even in challenging times there is still the opportunity to frame or reframe. In my challenge I chose to focus more on my survival than my suffering. Being optimistic is not easy but the reward is great. I was able to take something that was not good to me and turn it into something good for me, my family and my community. If I can be positive through all the storms, then so can you!

ABOUT THE AUTHOR

 Keisha Hawes is a wife, mother, Pastor and survivor.

She is a graduate of the College of Charleston with a degree in Urban Studies with a concentration in policy and social problems.

In May of 2011, Keisha, at age 31, survived a heart attack. In January 2013, Keisha attended the local American Heart Association Go Red for Women casting call to share her powerful story. She was chosen to be one of 11 women out of nearly 10,000 submitted as a national Go Red for Women spokesperson. She is the first American Heart Association spokesperson from South Carolina.

She is the Campus Pastor of Increasing Faith Christian Center, a member of Delta Theta Sorority, Inc., Alpha Phi Omega Fraternity, an active parent volunteer, and a frequent volunteer with many local organizations.

She lends her voice to make women and others aware of the risks, signs and symptoms of heart disease.

She is married to the love of her life, Michael, and the proud mother of three amazing children, Mason, Madison and Morrison. She is also the stepmother of three wonderful children.

To contact Keisha for speaking engagements or other opportunities, email her at wbhawes@gmail.com.

For more information, visit www.KeishaHawes.com

The Bravest Things I've Ever Done

Even though I now consider my children my greatest joys and accomplishments in life, for a large part of my life, I didn't want to be a mother. After experiencing sexual abuse as a child, I had no interest in bearing children. But life had other plans for me. My teenage boyfriend who beat me up several times was an alcoholic and drug addict, and we got pregnant just weeks before high school graduation. There was no question about what to do. I went off to college and a few weeks later got a safe and legal abortion without anyone else finding out. Though he stalked me for some time afterward, I was finally able to end the relationship and move on with my life. It was the lowest, darkest point of my life, and it's a good thing I didn't know that life could get even darker.

In my last year of college, I fell in love. I told him early in the relationship that I didn't want children, and I learned that he didn't either. We seemed perfect for each other. After a year-long engagement, we got married. Unfortunately we divorced three years later when he told me he'd been unfaithful.

A few years later I fell in love again and married. After a while the subject of children came up. We agreed we wanted children and started trying to get pregnant, but inside I was deeply afraid of the whole idea. When I didn't get pregnant right away, I thought maybe it was God's way of punishing me for getting an abortion and not wanting children for so long. This went on for a few years, and finally we decided to get fertility tests. I held my breath, secretly terrified that I would be cleared medically and some simple procedure would get us pregnant. So I consider this the first Bravest Thing I had ever done in my life: agreeing to have children.

It turned out to be a simple fertility problem that was easily solved. After one treatment, I was suddenly pregnant! I was so happy that I couldn't believe I was ever against it. But somehow it seemed too easy, like we had cheated somehow. That tiny voice of fear in the back of my mind warned me to beware.

Marisa

Everything went well through those early weeks of pregnancy. Although I was 38 years old, I was in overall good health. Still, the OB/GYN labeled me with four risk factors: obese, over 35, family history of miscarriages, and gestational diabetes. It meant I would have more frequent exams, which I thought was great. I wanted all the medical support I could get. Everything was progressing perfectly. We named our baby Marisa Isabella.

Then one morning in my 19th week, I woke up feeling nauseated and feverish. I didn't notice passing the pregnancy "plug," but, apparently, I had. Within a few hours, I had a raging fever. I called the doctor and she said to get to the hospital as soon as possible. By the time we got there, I was in labor.

In the emergency room, I was labeled as a potential miscarriage and sent to the maternity ward. They told my husband he could go on to work for his night shift but to come back in the morning. Things got pretty fuzzy after that. I remember being given medication and going to sleep. I have no real memory of the next few hours, just a very vague sense of someone sitting me up and telling me to push. Then I fell back to sleep.

Even before she was born, they already knew Marisa would not live; she was too small and had suffered brain hemorrhages due to my fever. But she was treated like any other preemie, taken to the NICU and bundled up in soft white blankets. She died naturally after about 45 minutes. When my husband returned after his shift, they woke me up and explained what had happened. My husband was angry and didn't understand. I was totally confused because I had no memory of her birth. They asked if we would like to talk to a grief counselor to help us deal with the situation, and we said yes.

Our grief counselor was an older woman with many years of experience. She explained where Marisa was and what had happened. Throughout the conversation, I found myself unable to believe that it was true. There had to be some mistake. I was sure Marisa was still alive and they had the wrong mom. Then I looked at my husband, and I saw something else in his eyes, something very different from what I was feeling. He was angry at me, like it was all my fault. In that moment, I knew it was true. She was gone.

The grief counselor offered us the opportunity to hold Marisa. She asked us to think hard about the fact that this would be our only chance to see her, ever, so we should take our time with the decision. At first, we both said no. We didn't want that to be our last, our only, memory of her. She then explained that it was hospital policy to cremate babies, and there would be no ashes to take home. She was making it clear that this really was our last chance to be with Marisa. So, we agreed. Then came the really hard part, which I will call the second Bravest Thing I've ever done, and it was quite a lot harder than the first one.

A few minutes later, a nurse brought her in and laid her in my arms. She was still warm, or at least the blankets were warm. I touched her face, her exquisite little fingers, and I lifted her tiny hand with my fingertip. Her eyes, her ears, her nose, all in miniature, were all infinitely perfect. We didn't talk much and just held her, touched her, and whispered her name. After a while, they came and took her. She was gone.

The rest is a blur. We chose cremation, and we signed papers. A while later, the grief counselor returned with a packet of materials, some photos of Marisa, and a little keepsake teddy bear. I was baffled by the photos, which showed her dressed in a tiny gown and a knitted preemie hat, cuddled in the arms of a handmade stuffed bunny. Who had taken the pictures? Had that person held her carefully, tenderly, when she dressed her? Was it done reverently and solemnly? Why couldn't I have done it?

The next day, we took the photos and the grief counseling information and left the hospital, without our Marisa. Years later, after the pain settled and softened enough, I bought a beautiful wooden box shaped like a book and put her things in it. Each year on her birthday, we open it and look at each thing and think about what age she would be, and what it might be like if she was with us. I saved and pressed a single flower from one of the arrangements that was sent to me. Apart from our memories of holding her in the hospital, that is all that was left.

There were no answers. It was just a time to be gotten through without reasons, explanations, or decisions. I moved through the motions of living, but I was lost inside. I had no anchor to anything that might have helped me cope. I simply existed, with no direction.

Then it was time to see the OBGYN again for a follow-up. I found her to be completely cold and unsympathetic. She told me that these things just happen and reminded about how 1 in 4 pregnancies end in miscarriage. She reviewed all my various risk factors, and added a fifth one, preterm labor. She made me realize that if I was going to try to get pregnant again, which I desperately wanted to do, I would need a more caring doctor.

I called the fertility doctor's office and explained what had happened with Marisa. I asked for help in finding a new doctor, someone highly qualified to work with someone with so many risk factors. The nurse said I should call the head of Obstetrics and Gynecology at the large teaching hospital nearby. So I gathered my courage and called him, the third Bravest Thing I've ever done. It was especially brave for me, since I have always been a people-pleaser, afraid of drawing attention to myself or making someone else uncomfortable. It was very hard for me to ask for help from anyone for anything, even something I desperately wanted. Deep inside, I was terrified of getting pregnant again, of facing more doctors with more questions and procedures and treatments, and of the same thing happening again.

The OB/GYN department head was very kind and understood exactly what I was going through. I asked him to recommend a new doctor for me, the best doctor he had trained in recent years. He immediately gave me the name of a doctor who had graduated number one in her medical school class and was one of the most gifted he had ever worked with. I was impressed. Anyone who could graduate first in her class meant she had taken everything seriously, every area of study, every class, every patient. My intuition told me she was the one.

Just the act of going through with that meeting and emerging with a name on a piece of paper, I felt like I could live again, that we could still have a baby. We started planning our next trip to the fertility doctor for another procedure. But somehow, miraculously, we got pregnant on our own.

Bianca

The news that I was pregnant again came as a shock to our family and friends. But they were as relieved and excited as we were. I had an amazing new OB/GYN who

I absolutely adored. The 1996 Olympics were set to start in July. It was a time of great patriotism and excitement, and my pregnancy progressed without incident. On July 19 I went to my 20-week ultrasound, excited to be able to see my baby on ultrasound.

My wonderful doctor was in the middle of the ultrasound when I saw her look suddenly at my vagina and then look again, very closely. Then she went absolutely still. I asked if everything was okay. She looked up calmly and smiled, and said "I think so, but I think I'll send you up to the hospital just to be sure." She patted my leg and walked casually out of the room.

Within a few minutes, the urgency of the situation hit me. It was opening day of the Olympics, and the governor had ordered all the interstates closed except to emergency traffic. I was one of the emergencies, tearing up the interstate toward the hospital at 90 mph. Had the roads been open, I would likely have had my second miscarriage in the back of that ambulance in rush hour traffic.

At the hospital, I was quickly admitted, put in a special birthing room, and hooked up to monitors and an IV. My bed was tilted into what's called Trendelenburg position, with my head lower than my feet. The purpose of it was to put my uterus in the most relaxed position possible and take pressure off the cervix. I realized I was at almost the exact same point in my pregnancy that I was when I lost Marisa, so something similar must be happening.

About an hour later, my doctor arrived and explained what was going on. When she was doing that routine ultrasound in her office, she had seen my daughter's tiny fingers in the birth canal. I was dilating and effacing, and the thin membrane of the amniotic sac was all that was keeping Bianca safe inside me. There was only a small window of time to save us from another preterm birth, and she had done it. She was my hero, then and forever. I cried for hours.

I was a model patient, doing everything the various specialists asked of me with the greatest care and attention to detail. It was the only way I could keep down the panic. They said don't leave the hospital bed, don't move around too much, don't even raise up, don't brush my waist length hair. Everything had to be done in that tilted position, which made everything harder. When they told me I would have to have a routine minor surgery, I didn't even think twice.

The surgery turned out to be a bit painful since I couldn't have anesthesia. The doctors decided to give my cervix some extra help in staying closed, so they sewed me closed with a "purse-string" cerclage. And just to make it really strong, they put in two. That increased my confidence that we could go full term, but I still had to stay in the declined position. Thankfully the Olympics were on TV all day every day, and that helped distract me from my ordeal. Then the horrible Olympic Park bombing happened, and I watched as the rest of the world dealt with that terrible event and I lay immobile in my bed.

As the weeks passed, I began to miss home terribly. I wanted my own bed, my cat, my garden, my life with my husband. I begged and pleaded to just go home for a weekend or even a day. Just for a break from the hospital. Finally, after six weeks in that horrible tilted hospital bed, my doctor agreed, but with strict instructions about what I could and could not do.

Later that same day, I overdid it. I was sweeping my kitchen when a vaguely familiar tug started in my lower abdomen. I knew that feeling from what happened with Marisa. I called the doctor, and my husband immediately took me back to the hospital. I was in labor again. They started new medications to stave off labor and steroids to speed up Bianca's development, and I experienced a deep slump in my motivation. I still had a long way to go, to make it to the point where she could survive. We aimed for at least 33 weeks. It was only week 26. I settled into hospital life again.

Finally on the first day of October, around 9 a.m., I was laying there totally aggravated by the noise of LifeFlight helicopters landing outside my window. I gritted my teeth and tried to roll onto my side and curl up in a ball against the sound. It was only my 29th week; I could not imagine being like that for three more weeks! Then I felt a strange sensation in my belly and I knew that my water had broken. I called the nurse and started on the roller coaster ride toward emergency C-section surgery and delivery.

They brought in an anesthesiologist who tried to insert an epidural in my spine. I was so weak, I could barely sit up to allow him good access to my back. Seconds later we went into the operating room, my husband with me and holding my hand. I began to get concerned during all the prep that I still had feeling in my legs and feet. The epidural was not working!

As they began to strap my arms down, pure panic started rising in my chest. I begged for them to wait, I was not numb! But the process was under way and they would not, could not stop. I tried as hard as I could to contain my terror, but I think I screamed as the first scalpel cut into my abdomen. A nurse tried to give me a dose of valium through the IV in my arm, but it did nothing to mask the searing pain in my belly. I looked over at my IV and noticed that the white tape holding it was no longer sticking to my arm. I called again to a nurse to check it, and when she looked closer, she saw that the tip of the IV needle was no longer in the vein. There was no time to do anything else for me. It was an all-out emergency now focused on saving my baby, and I would have to endure whatever happened, with no anesthesia.

I'll spare you the details of what it's like to feel a C-section. It took tremendous courage to accept what was happening, and it was undoubtedly the fourth Bravest Thing I have ever done. I did it for my baby, Bianca, and for Marisa. I was willing to go through anything to ensure that Bianca would survive. My OB/GYN did her best to keep me calm throughout the whole ordeal, and she apologized profusely afterward. When Bianca was finally lifted out of my body, I was not even aware of the pain anymore, listening only for the sound of her breathing and waiting for the sight of her tiny body. One glimpse, one vigorous wail, and she was hurried out of the room.

Though born at only 29 weeks, she was the size of a 33-week baby. I learned how to use the industrial strength breast pump, and soon I was pumping and storing the colostrum and sending it off with a nurse every few hours. The nurses made over me like I was some kind of celebrity, but in the NICU they treated Bianca like a queen! There were many babies in there much worse off than she was.

Every sort of neonatal specialist visited her daily. We were cautioned about all sorts of possible complications of her prematurity, from blindness to holes in her heart or intestines to lung problems. I kept pumping breastmilk and bringing it in each day even after I went home. She was growing beautifully and showing every sign of perfect health.

Bianca finally left the hospital at 6 weeks old and 4 pounds, 7 ounces, bright and strong and beautiful. She thrived and was a joy to care for, an easy baby with a bright personality. She crawled at 8 months and stood up at one year a couple of days before she cut her first tooth. Our new normal gradually came together and we all grew into our new life as a family.

Orlando

Surprisingly, it wasn't long before we were talking about our next baby. We hoped to have a son. I had suggested Bianca's name, so we decided that he would name our next baby. In a moment of intuition before I was even pregnant again, he declared that the following month I would become pregnant with a boy, and we would name him Orlando Leonardo. And that is exactly how it happened!

This time, my wonderful OB/GYN was sure she had me figured out, and she convinced me of that, too. I went into this third pregnancy in four years confident and ready to take on whatever happened.

About halfway through the pregnancy, I developed gestational diabetes. I had put on weight with each pregnancy and had not lost any. I had to start taking insulin, which was scary to me, handling needles and keeping things sterile and such. I listened intently as my doctor described the two kinds of insulin, how much and when to take them, and what they did in my body.

By the time I filled the prescriptions at my neighborhood pharmacy, I had calmed down and felt in control of the situation. But that afternoon, when I went to take the first mealtime dose, the fear of doing something wrong suddenly resurfaced. I carefully picked up the bottle, read the pharmacy label, and drew out 50 units of insulin. But something about that number seemed wrong. That was not the dose I had discussed with my doctor. It was way off, like ten times the dose she described! I checked the label again, the directions, the syringe -- everything looked right, but I *knew* it was wrong.

So then I did my final very Bravest Thing, the last one in this story. I called the pharmacist and I told him I

104

thought he had made a mistake. I don't think I had ever challenged someone in authority like that in my whole life, so it took all of the courage I could muster! Suddenly he said, "Have you injected it yet?" with great urgency. I said no, and he said "Don't use it! I did make a mistake!" He was looking at the doctor's paper prescription in front of him, and there in her neat, clear handwriting was the dose, 5 units. He had added a zero, making it 50 units, an error that might well have killed me and Orlando both. Later I learned it was an error that occurred so often, it prompted a nationwide change in how doctors write insulin prescriptions.

Compared to the ease with which he was brought into the world (a painless C-section and extended recovery period in the hospital), raising my infant Orlando was full of challenges completely unlike those I faced with Bianca. First, he was huge! He looked like a miniature defensive end. By the time he had his first birthday, he was almost as big as Bianca, and yet she was two years older. People actually wondered if they were twins! Second, he nursed; oh did he nurse. Bianca had been too small to nurse, which is why I used the breast pump. Orlando nursed so much he gained two pounds in his first week. It was a relief when he started taking cereal in his bottles, which satisfied his hunger longer. He grew so fast, we nicknamed him "the incredible Hulk baby"!

Thankfully the rest of the story of my children is a happy one, with all the normal ups and downs. Bringing them into the world was the hard part, and it required a tremendous amount of bravery. But I wonder now how I ever could have *not* wanted children. Looking back on it, the difficulties were easily outweighed by the joy of nurturing them and watching them grow. They were wonderful, fun and easy to raise and great playmates for each other. I guess my greatest fear was that I would not measure up to motherhood. Old feelings of shame and guilt clouded my mind and made me feel unworthy. But the whole experience made me realize that I was most definitely worthy. I was willing to do anything to ensure their health and safety. Despite what I once thought, I am far braver than I ever could have imagined, and motherhood is far more fulfilling than I ever could have dreamed!

ABOUT THE AUTHOR

Camilla Herold is a 61-year-old mother, wife, writer, artist, and healer from Summerville, South Carolina, who is dedicated to helping survivors of sexual trauma. By speaking out about her own experiences, she hopes to raise awareness and provide support and comfort to those still suffering. She believes that through the powers of intuition, an open heart, a reverence for nature, and authentic relationships with our fellow humans, all trauma can be healed. She plans to release her memoir in 2019, followed closely by a second book on healing from trauma through a focus on body, mind, soul, and spirit.

You can contact Camilla at camilla.lapaz@gmail.com.

I Changed the Course of My Life

I was working in my dream job at my dream company. I loved going to work every day. I loved my co-workers, I loved our customers, I loved everything. I was surrounded by people who had been at the company for 10, 20, even 30 years and their loyalty knew no bounds. I wanted to be one of them. I wanted to be a lifer, too. I never even thought about finding another job. I was in my early thirties and knew I had found my corporate forever home.

When they announced the restructuring, I honestly didn't pay that much attention. They were just shuffling responsibilities at the top of the company -- again. I had been with the company five years and we had gone through a restructuring at least three times, so I knew there was would some temporary upheaval, but it was all be fine.

But this time, it wasn't.

My division was now under the direction of a newly-hired Senior Vice President (SVP). I didn't know that much about him. He had only been with the company a short time when the restructuring took place.

Looking back, I should have asked more questions as to why one of his first decisions was to eliminate the position of the woman who was out on maternity leave. She was the Director of Operations and was one of only three director-level females in the company. Her responsibilities were going to be absorbed by the Senior Manager of Operations who had been there 30+ years. Within three months, the Senior Manager announced his retirement. There were only two staff members who reported directly to him and neither of them had any interest in taking over the job.

I wasn't in Operations. I was in the Marketing Department as the Senior Copywriter/Assistant Art Director. But in my role, I was a linchpin. I made sure that all marketing materials and copy for any reason was created up to brand standards. We ran six major marketing campaigns a year for our main product, and another five or six for our ancillary products, and each campaign would have up to 30 variations. We were also in the throes of implementing a new internal fulfillment system, which meant that every single bill sent to a customer, every renewal letter, every customer service template, etc., had to be reviewed and rewritten to work in the new systems.

When the job posting for the Manager of Operations was posted, I applied and was politely told "no, you don't have the qualifications" by human resources. And there were things in the description that I had never done, so I accepted it. Besides, I was happy where I was. But as the search to fill those open positions dragged on, I began to be invited to meetings with IT and outside consultants. The two operations staff would come to me to review bids from potential new suppliers. When something went awry in a product delivery, I was getting the call. Both the remaining Operations staff members were terrified of the new SVP. He was harsh and demanding and they left in tears after meeting with him.

Then one of them quit.

Now the company was in a bind because a crucial area of the company was basically unstaffed. I had been the only internal applicant to the job, so even though they thought I was unqualified, they offered me the job of Manager of Operations. On the organization chart, they had me reporting to a Senior Manager, who reported to a Director, who reported to a Senior Director, who reported to the Senior Vice President. All the positions between me and SVP were vacant.

I dove into the job with gusto because I was going to prove that I was qualified for the job. I gave it my all. I was often the first person in the building in the morning, and usually the last person to leave at night. I had charts and lists and was super organized and I could tell you where every moving part was at any given moment. I kept a tight rein on the budgets and I didn't let problems linger. If something was going wrong, I wanted a solution.

One of the problems I discovered when I took over Operations was their lack of expense tracking. There was a yearly budget created in November for the next year. No one was tracking how we were doing compared to budget monthly. Accounting was doing it at a high level, but those reports were only shared with upper management. I felt like I needed to know how the money was being spent.

I had developed a template for tracking and projecting expenses in Marketing so we could monitor how much we were paying outside artists versus our internal staff (to justify hiring more staff, honestly) that had made our budgeting process a breeze. (While I was there, Marketing was always the first department to get our budgets submitted and we were always right on target on our numbers.) I started using the same template for everything done in Operations. The next thing I knew, the entire company was using my template. Only it wasn't "my" template, it was supposedly the idea of SVP.

That soon became a pattern. He took credit for everything. I negotiated a big discount with a new supplier – he would claim that he negotiated the deal. I came up with an idea for a new script book for customer service, it was an idea he had brought with him from a previous company. I suggested we turn an empty office into a meeting room so I didn't have to go to the conference room clear on the other side of the building to meet with suppliers. As the desk was removed and a conference table installed, other department heads are giving him high-fives for having such a great idea.

SVP had a very sharp tongue and could cuss you out like nobody else. He was not a nice guy to be around if he was angry or annoyed. If you had a thin skin, then you didn't want to make a mistake because he was relentless in his criticism. And he would berate you just standing in the cubicle field where everyone could hear. And if something went wrong, it was always someone else's fault. He was never to blame. He would claim to have told me to take care of something, and when I didn't, I was the one not following up.

No one was qualified for their jobs. Everyone was lazy. Everyone was careless. Stupid was his favorite word. But put him in a room with the Board of Directors, other Vice Presidents and outside consultants, he was charming and witty. And because he took credit for everything, he was considered this golden boy-wonder. He knew how to play the political game.

I developed very thick skin. He could call me a "B," he could call me stupid, he could yell at me for 15 minutes straight and I didn't let it in. I knew I was giving it my best effort. I knew the truth of what I had done or not done. He once called me lazy and I stopped him dead in his tracks. "Do you really believe what you just said? Do you know anyone who works harder than I do? Tell me who." His retort: "Well, you aren't lazy, but just because you work hard doesn't mean you are doing your job." I just couldn't win. And there was never an apology.

I quickly learned that if I took ownership of a mistake, whether I had done it or not, it would de-fuse the situation. Once I said "I'm sorry. I should have..." and didn't respond by getting angry or defensive, he calmed down. Other staff members marveled at how I could take the abuse.

In this Operations role, I had the Billing and Renewals Coordinator (with two to four staff members), and the Manager of Lists (with two subordinates) and my three assistants reporting to me. I cannot tell you how many times I would return from a meeting to find someone in tears waiting for me. I couldn't keep an assistant. They all told me the same thing, "It's not you. You're a great boss. But we can't keep working here because of him." The atmosphere was toxic.

There were days when I wanted to quit. Honestly, there were days that I probably should have quit because it was nothing but abuse. But I stayed. Sometimes I told myself I was staying because I couldn't just abandon my staff. They could leave me, but I couldn't leave them. Sometimes I told myself I was staying because I was doing a great job, and someone was going to notice it eventually. There would be a particularly bad day and for the next few weeks I'd send out a dozen resumes. But nothing came my way. I felt stuck.

The search for a Director of Operations was always ongoing. The candidates would come in, meet with Human Resources, then with SVP and a couple other executives, and then I would be invited to meet with them. There was one candidate who was a complete jerk, very dismissive, very know-it-all in his interview. When SVP asked what I thought, I told him I thought he was rude and arrogant. SVP replied, "That's exactly why I like him. He would keep you and your staff in line." I just shook my head. I was sure he would be hired any day. I was relieved when he was not offered the position.

The company overall had a great year. We set sales records, we lowered costs, everything was humming. There were new hires in many departments, we were getting prepared for an even better year to come.

I was given a task to create a report for the executives and Board of Directors to show why we had had such a great year. I was given all the corporate financial reports and summaries from all departments. One of the things that jumped out to me quickly was how much my department was under budget in terms of personnel. But that made sense on the surface because I knew the Director position was open. But as I looked closer, I saw that another department was significantly over budget in their personnel costs and they had recently hired a new manager. This new hire was a young man right out of grad school with no work experience. And if I was doing my math right, it looked like he was hired making about $20,000 more than I was.

I was dumbfounded. I thought I was making a good salary. I didn't think I had a reason to complain about money. But this guy, with no experience, was making more than I was after being there for almost eight years.

I felt I needed an explanation. But I didn't want to come across as a complainer because I knew how that would go over. So, I created a new organization chart for my department. I proposed that I be promoted to the Director position with a decent raise, promote some of my staff, re-distribute some of the responsibilities and still stay in budget. Honestly, I thought it was a good, solid plan.

I went to my boss' office toward the end of the day. I had been rehearsing my pitch to him for days. I got maybe three minutes into it and he stopped me. "Just stop," he said. "I see where you think this is going but I'm just going to be honest with you. It's never going to happen."

"Why not?" I said. "I really think..." and he cut me off again.

"Listen to me. You aren't going to be promoted again. You were just promoted two years ago. You are too young for the responsibility you have now, and you only got the job because you were the only one who applied. You are a female, which means you aren't even going to be looked at for another promotion until you're forty, and besides, you don't have an advanced degree."

I was stunned. I tried to raise a rebuttal, but it was no use. He lectured me for another ten minutes or so about why I was unworthy. That young man who was hired at a higher salary? He had his MBA and was married and was in a completely different department. Why would I think I was as valuable as him? He had a future in the company. I didn't. I should just be grateful and not rock the boat. Maybe he could rearrange things to give me more responsibility (like I didn't have enough on my plate!) and see if he could get me my yearly raise a little early, but he couldn't make any promises.

I went home defeated. But I was also angry. When I finished crying, I thought about what he said. Age, gender and an advanced degree were the obstacles he had placed before me. I couldn't do anything about my age. I couldn't do anything about my gender. But that advanced degree? Now that I could do something about.

I started researching Master of Business Administration programs. There was no part-time MBA program at the Ohio State University or any other local colleges. I would have to quit my job and go to school full-time. That just didn't sound appealing to me. I had just purchased my first home and didn't think I could afford to quit working.

There were some online MBA programs, like the College of Phoenix, but they were new, didn't have the best reputations and were generally frowned upon by most human resources departments. When I looked at the actual curriculums, I felt I would be bored to tears. I mean, I was marketing and strategic planning every day. I didn't need to take a class and do a project on it in my spare time.

Then one day I was online and pulled up a list of graduate degrees and I saw the juris doctorate – the J.D. I could go to law school. Ding-ding-ding! That might be interesting. It was certainly different than what I was doing every day. I considered it to be an even "better" degree than an MBA. I mean, how many of the executives at my company had MBAs? Almost all of them. But how many had a law degree? I only knew of one -- the human resources director.

I decided to go to law school.

I kept the decision quiet. I didn't tell anyone when I took the LSAT. In fact, I drove to Toledo to take it because I was afraid someone I knew might see me if I took it at Ohio State. I didn't tell anyone when I applied to two different law schools and got accepted into both. I chose the night school program through Capital University School of Law where I could attend classes Monday through Thursday from 6 p.m. until 10 p.m. for four years. The campus was about a 40-minute drive from my office during rush hour traffic, so I knew I would have to leave around 5 p.m. every day.

I didn't tell my co-workers when I sent in my first tuition payment or went to orientation weekend. In fact, the first week of class, I calmly picked up my stuff and left the office at 5 p.m. without saying anything to anyone. The first day or two, no one thought anything of it. By the third day, one of my assistants asked me what was going on because I was leaving so early (which was the time everyone else was leaving but it was early for me). I told her I was taking a class but didn't mention what sort of class.

It was almost a month later when my boss approached me and asked why I kept leaving early. He had given me a task late in the day and expected it to be done before I went home and here I was gathering my things and walking out the door. I told him I had enrolled in law school. He replied by telling me it was ridiculous. And he told me that he hoped it wouldn't interfere with my job, with all that studying and stuff, and reminded me that he expected certain deadlines to be met. I needed to make sure my job was my priority.

Two days later, the Director of Human Resources came to my cubicle and asked me to come see him after lunch. I thought I was going to be fired.

I wasn't fired. But the Director was concerned because he heard I was attending law school. He asked me point-blank if my intention was to sue the company for harassment. He said he had been receiving complaint after complaint about my boss and hearing stories about how awful the situation was. I gave him my opinion. He took some notes, asked some questions, and nodded a lot.

Shortly thereafter, my boss was reassigned to a position with no one reporting to him and I got a new boss. This boss wasn't toxic, but by then, I was hooked on law school. I absolutely loved my classes and classmates. I continued to work at my company while I went to school, eventually working out an agreement where I could work part-time.

When I graduated from law school and passed the bar, I left my job and used my corporate world experience to start my own law firm. It wasn't easy, but I had no desire to continue to work in a corporate environment.

One of my first major cases was to represent a female employee in a harassment case against a local bank. I realized then that I could have sued my employer, and probably would have won, but I let it go.

That decision to go to law school took my life in a whole new direction. I made a sharp left turn onto a path I had never envisioned. I was too afraid to just quit and take that leap, but I took a step to change my situation. I earned that advanced degree. I focused on creating a new future. I took the abuse but knew that I wouldn't be there forever. I knew I had more worth than was acknowledged at that job.

And without that sharp left turn, I would have had a completely different life. There's no way to know if it would have been better or worse, but I know some of the most important people in my life came through my law school experience. And being an attorney for ten years brought me to a place to truly understand my true purpose here on earth.

If you are in a toxic environment, just know that the true issue is with them, not you. Continue to do your best and keep your eyes and ears open for new opportunities.

ABOUT THE AUTHOR

 Katryna Johnson, J.D., aka Trina, is the owner of Mirelli Entrepreneur Training for Women, a women's organization bringing powerful like-minded women who want to learn, connect, grow and prosper together through one-on-one coaching, workshops, conferences, networking events, collaborations and more. Her passion for helping women achieve came out of seeing many of her law clients broken and demoralized after divorce. She began helping them build confidence, take responsibility for their lives, and launch businesses.

To learn more about Mirelli, visit http://Mirellietc.com.

She is also the co-founder of Amazing Speaks, an international speaker training company helping women create their speaking platforms, hone their public speaking skills, and get on stages to share their messages.

To learn more about Amazing Speaks, visit http://AmazingSpeaks.com.

She is a graduate of The Ohio State University with a Bachelor's of the Arts in Journalism and a Juris Doctorate from Capital University Law School.

To contact her for speaking engagements, email her at Trina@Mirellietc.com or call 843-824-4025.

I Always Find a Way to Grow

I have been struggling with how to go about this project. You see, I was given a simple task, if you think about it. I suppose for most people it would be easy to just tell your story. For me on the other hand it's not as simple as picking a time and place in my life that I felt was that defining moment, that moment when everything became so clear to me that I knew the exact direction I had to take. How can I possibly describe such a moment to you if I'm still trying to figure that out myself?

Therefore; I have decided that I would give you some highlights of my life and let you decide which circumstance of my life you feel would define the person I am today.

I was born to an 18-year-old single woman who suddenly realized she was five months into her pregnancy. She made several attempts to abort but she was not successful in finding someone to end the pregnancy (and yes, she told me this story herself). My birth was not by any means a normal one. I was a large nine-and-a-half-pound baby that was breech. The doctors decided not to do a c-section and to let me come into the world showing off my buddy (I suppose I can blame them for having such a big one).

I became very familiar with hospital settings. I had eight pneumonias before the age of eight and I would spend weeks and sometimes months in the hospital at a time.

I was raised in a black family. I had a black daddy whom I called Pipo. I loved him dearly and he gave me nothing but love in return. I also had a black grandmother, as well as black aunts and cousins. Really only me and my mom where the white ones in that family. But I truly thought nothing of it because I was a very happy child surrounded by love.

I was five when my mother decided we would go live with my Abuela at her little ranch. All I can tell you about the tiny ranch is that there were eight of us living in a one-bedroom house. Only a small part of the house had concrete floors, the kitchen and the bathroom. The other two rooms (living room and bedroom) had dirt floors. The bedroom had two bunk beds and a full-size bed. The living room also had two bunk beds. My brother and I shared one, and my two youngest uncles shared the other.

For the most part I was happy there. I was the only girl in a house full of boys. My Abuela was so happy to have me around, since her first child was the only girl (my mom) and then she was followed by six brothers. I was her little girl. I remember her sitting me on the front porch of the house after I would take a shower and making curls in my hair for hours at a time. I lived there from the age of five until I was seven. We were poor, but we were happy.

At some point during my stay there my second-to-youngest uncle, who was around sixteen at the time, snuck into my bed one night and did things I was not okay with. After that one incident he made me a promise he would never do it again if I didn't tell anyone (so I didn't, until I was thirty years old).

At the age of six my mother took me to meet a strange man, who drove up in his motorcycle. They told me he was my biological father. I had a lot of questions after that visit. Wait, what? So, if you're my dad, who is the other guy that has been in my life until now? Why was Pipo not my father? Where the hell have you been for the last six years? None of my questions got answered. I was only informed that they had decided to get back together and form a family. (Wait, I already have a family. Who are you again?)

A year later they took me to my new home and introduced me to my new family. Suddenly I had another grandmother and grandfather (I never had one of those before, since my mom's dad had left Cuba when I was born). I also had new aunts, uncles and three girl cousins. Apart from my youngest uncle and my new Grandpa, everyone else treated me like an outsider.

When I was nine-years-old my parents told my brother and me that we had no choice but to move again. We were going to the United States. (Where is that? And why are you taking me there? I don't want to leave, I have new friends now.) I was leaving with my new family and had to leave my old family behind (my Abuela and my Pipo).

My uncle Tony met us when our boat got to Key West. He had arrived ten months before us. I was so happy to see him. At last someone familiar who I liked and who liked me.

My new life in the United States presented many challenges. First, I didn't understand anything the other kids would say to me or about me. However, God always grants us that intuition of knowing when people are making fun of us. Sometimes, I wish he had not done that. It's very hard to get over how cruel kids can be.

Shortly after we arrived, my grandfather started to feel bad. He spent so much time in hospitals I barely got to spend any time with him anymore. Eight months later, he passed away and once again I was lonely. Although I had many people around me all the time, I always felt that emptiness of not having anyone who understood me.

Grandpa made a small appearance after his passing. One night while I accompanied my grandmother in his old bed, he showed up, sat at the edge of the bed and just watched over me. I never told anyone because I was afraid they would say I was crazy, so I convinced myself was all a dream.

As a matter of a fact after that incident I decided not to speak at all, period. For the next few years I kept to myself and barely said a word to anyone. Even when I had something to say I stumbled on my words, so to keep myself from being humiliated, I decided it was best to be quiet.

When I was eleven a group of child psychologists came by to observe us at my elementary school in Los Angeles, California. They went to speak to my parents and I was told I needed special classes. So, I would go into school an hour before anyone else to learn my ABC's and shortly regained my voice again.

I suppose I must have accumulated a lot to say during those two years, because I haven't stop talking ever since. I will say what's on my mind, whether you like it or not. If I have something to say It will burst out. It's a work in progress. During our four years of living in California (we moved there when my grandpa passed away), we moved two times and I went to two elementary schools and one middle school. My father's drinking increased as the years went by, as did his mental and physical abuse towards my mother and us.

When I was fourteen, my parents moved us back to sunny Florida. Again, we moved a lot. We moved four times and I went to three different high schools in a two-year period. No, we were not in the military, my parents just didn't budget the rent payments and we continuously had to find another place to go.

Our last home in Alappata, on the North West side, Miami, was the worst of them all. There were constant strangers coming in and out of our house. To walk into my new school, I had to go through metal detectors and had my purse opened by police officers in uniforms. There were chain-link fenced hallways and the outside fence was blocks. It felt more like a prison then a school. For the most part kids there didn't go to learn anything, and the teachers didn't teach because they spent most of their time and effort breaking up fights and keeping the order in the classroom.

One day I woke up early to go to school and opened my parent's bedroom door to give my little brother a kiss. (My mom had forgotten to lock the door.) There was a pile, almost a mountain, of white power on top of my parent's dresser with a small weigh machine next to it. "What is this?" I asked myself. Then, suddenly, everything started making sense to me and I knew exactly what I needed to do.

I packed my bookbag with as many clothes as I could stuff in it. I took the school bus and asked someone if I could use their phone. I called my boyfriend at the time and asked him to pick me up.

"I left my house and I'm never going back," I said to him. "So if you are still willing to marry me, you better come and pick me up now."

I finished high school at night and was able to graduate on time even though I had a full-time job babysitting during the day. Four years into the marriage, at age twenty, I had my first child. She was everything I had dreamed. God had finally granted me something that was mine and I was not going to let anything, or anyone, hurt her like they had with me. My dream of going to college was put on hold, but never forgotten.

One night only four months after she was born, I was rocking her in her room trying to alleviate her colic. I was so tired that night from having had very little sleep and exhausted from so many sleepless nights. I could feel my eyes heavy and my arms starting to let her go, when I suddenly woke back up. I then decided it would be best to take her to my bed, so I wouldn't drop her. Her father woke up screaming and demanding for me to shut her up. He got out of bed and reached to grab her. It was at that exact moment when I took her away from him that I decided it was time to let him and the marriage go.

Once again, I found myself lonely. But, this time I was not alone. I was responsible for another person's life and I was determined to give her the best life possible. Shortly after moving into my small one-bedroom apartment where my baby's crib didn't fit, a new man walked into my life and started helping me with the baby and with things that needed to get done around the house. He was a great friend, but the relationship evolved and before I realized it I was pregnant with my second child. We married before our son was born and were divorced before he turned one.

One Sunday evening, we were driving home from a birthday party, my children were tightly tucked in their child restraint seats. I entered the intersection with a green light and all I could remember was a car heading straight at me. I hit the brakes as hard as I could, everything slowed down like in slow motion. I heard a very hard noise, but everything sounded like it was far away.

Finally, I must have come back to my senses because I could hear people next to me. Somehow, I had ended up under the hood of my car. I wanted to see my children, but I could not move, and I could not see them. Everyone around me kept telling me they were fine but all I kept asking was, "Please I need to see them." Finally, a police officer came over and took them out of their car seats and brought them to the front of the car. Within a few minutes of seeing them, I realized I could not feel anything from my waist down.

Oh my God, I was paralyzed. Why couldn't I move? A few minutes later the sirens got closer and closer. The paramedics explained to me that the only way they could take me out from under the hood was to put a plastic stretcher under my body and pull me out carefully. A few minutes after agreeing to the process, I was out from my trap and my blood started circulating again and I felt the most excruciating pain imaginable.

After a nine-hour surgery on my right leg and several days in the hospital I was ready to go home. When the doctor made his rounds that morning, he said to me "You know it will be at least eight months before you can walk again. In the meantime, since you had so many wounds and we couldn't put a cast on, the right leg cannot touch the floor."

A new chapter started in my life, one where I had to depend on other people for everything. Suddenly I had no legs to sustain me, no job, no income, no car and I was about to lose my house and my sanity.

One day I had an idea, and the next day I asked my brother (who is handy) to come over. We added a wall kitchen between my kitchen and family room and divided the home in two. I added a kitchen to the back side and rented it for almost the amount of my mortgage. My boss gave me unemployment since he didn't have any handicap access and I was not able to get into the office with my wheelchair.

After only six months of excruciating pain, endless hours of therapy at a clinic and at home, I was ready to take my life back. When I came home everyone kept asking me, "So how do you want to celebrate tonight?" I said, "I want to go dancing," and so we did.

That night I met husband number three. He helped me by taking care of my children after work while I went to school at night. Two years later, when I was almost at the end of my associate degree in accounting, I got pregnant. I had to stop going to school because my child was sitting very low and I needed bed rest after an eight-hour work day. School was put on the back burner again. Only a month after my little girl was born, I got a phone call from the school. It had been six months since I had taken a class and if I didn't register for the new semester, they would have to drop me from the school. So, what could I do? I had to go back to work and school only 30 days after giving birth because I was determined to do something with my life.

After twelve years of mental abuse and being isolated from everyone in my life I decided again to start a new life. After a year of separation and endless court battles, I was once again free. I felt like a butterfly all over again. I walked away with nothing because I felt I needed to buy my freedom, and I did.

Then one night I went dancing again (I haven't stopped dancing ever again) and I met my new love -- someone who was loving and caring for his children and mother. We have been together ever since. Although I must say as with all marriages, we've had our ups and downs, for the most part we've live a very good and happy life together.

Two years ago, after 25 years in corporate America I decided I was tired of working for other people and had to find my own way. It has not been easy, especially since my husband has not been supportive of my decision. At times I have felt that he is holding me back. I'm mostly upset because when we first met, I supported him while he went to school fulltime for three years. Not having that support at home has been hard. After months of questioning whether I had made the right choice, I started reaching out to other women entrepreneurs' groups around the area. I feel I have built a great support team that I know I can count on, and for this I am forever thankful.

As you can see it's very hard to pinpoint a moment and a time where I evolved into the person I am today. Somewhere along the way, my struggles, my tears, my laughter and my joy have made me into the women I am today. Still evolving, still finding herself and ready to do it all over again.

My journey has taught me many things: First, there is nothing that you set your mind to that you cannot accomplish; second, that no matter how hard the situation can feel now there is always tomorrow; and Third and most importantly, no matter how lonely I have felt at times, somehow, I always knew that God and my angels were there holding me. My faith carried me through.

I encourage each and everyone one of you to live the life that you deserve to have. Learn from your mistakes but not to dwell on them because life will always give you a new opportunity. To help others along the way, believe me, it has rewards. Whatever you set out to do in life, do it with passion or don't do it at all. Give yourselves the opportunities to evolve. Just like everything around us changes, we should to. Love yourself enough to take the time to get to know who you are. But most of all forgive... forgive yourself... and forgive those along the way who harmed you.

ABOUT THE AUTHOR

 Iskra Perez-Salcedo was born in Cuba and came to the US at the age of nine during the 1980 Mariel Exodus. Education has always played a big part of her vision, since it was through education that she broke away from poverty levels and gave her three children better opportunities.

After twenty-five years of a very successful career in accounting, her corporate International Financial Analyst position was eliminated.

The life she had built for herself had collapsed. So at the age of 45, she looked around and saw no job, her kids had moved out, and discovered herself in a deep depression. She suddenly found herself spending more and more time alone and she consistently putting on weight.

It was then that she decided it was time to reinvent her path. She started a new healthier lifestyle and has lost a total of 60 lbs. She is currently the CEO of IPS Accounting Services, a company providing multiple services optimizing growth for businesses.

To learn more about her accounting and business services, visit IPSAccountingServices.com

She also took her lifelong hobby of event design and turned it into a side business, Charleston Events Design, creating unique and memorable moments is a great outlet for her creativity and social engagements.

In addition, she founded the first Hispanic women entrepreneur's group in Charleston. Hispanic Women Entrepreneurs of South Carolina is a self-development group founded to help Hispanic women develop their leadership skills as they build and expand their relationships in their community through training, motivation, and collaboration.

To contact Iskra for speaking engagements, please send an email to iskrap@ipsaccountingservices.com.

I Am Not a Product of
My Environment

Growing up in the District of Columbia was not easy. I grew up in heavily crime-infested areas like South East, North East, South West and North West. My mom was an alcoholic and I never knew my dad. My mom told me she met my dad in Michigan when she was in her twenties. He was just visiting, and she met him at a party. She slept with him the first night they met, and she got pregnant. She said she saw him a little bit after that and told him that she was pregnant, but of course he said that I wasn't his child. She found out later that he had other kids that she was unaware of at the time.

Knowing that my dad didn't want me or have anything to do with me put a big empty place in my life. I was longing to know my dad and who he was, but I never got the chance. I started to ask questions like "Why didn't he want me?" and "Why didn't he love me?" I started to look for love in all the wrong places trying to fill that void in my heart. I thought if someone showed me some attention then that meant they loved me. That was so far from the truth. But I didn't care at the time because I was seeking the love I was missing from both of my parents.

My mom tried to be a good mom at first. But life happened to her. She started to drink more and more so I had to grow up fast to take care of my sister who is four years younger than me. I didn't know how to do that. Here I am 12 years old and I am having to take on the responsibilities of an adult. My mom would leave the house at different hours of the night leaving me to care for my sister. She would bring different men home. Some of them were ones she invited, others were not. My sister and I had to watch my mom get beat up by her boyfriends and even raped by guys she didn't know.

One day, one of her boyfriends (who I really didn't care for) saw me at a store and approached me. He told me to get in his car. I didn't want to, but I did. I was so scared of what he would do to my mom, my sister and me if I didn't do what he said. He asked me "What do men have?" That is not a question you would ask a child and I wouldn't answer him. He said that if I didn't say it he would hit me, so I said it. Then once we got home he tried to touch me. I told my mom and she didn't believe me. I couldn't believe what I was hearing! My own mom didn't believe me, her own daughter. I was so hurt and confused. The person who ended up believing me and had him removed from the home was my mom's friend at the time.

Throughout the years my mom continuously was abused. I hated to see her go through that, but I didn't know what to do. I had my own issues. I was getting bullied everyday throughout elementary and junior high school because of the way I looked and dressed. I was skinny and had to wear clothes that were given to us.

I would escape to television. I thought that if I pretended that I was somewhere else or someone else that all that stuff would go away. But it didn't. I had to endure people telling me that I was nothing, I will never be nothing and that I would never have anything.

At the age of 12, I got a job selling cookies and candy to make some money because my mom started not letting me use stuff in the house. I worked that job until I was 16 and was able to get a job at McDonald's. I worked there for a few years and then worked many other jobs. Every year I kept telling myself that there was something better out there for me. I told myself I didn't want to go through everything that my mom went through.

In high school I had a mentor, Ms. Norris. I will never forget her saying that "you don't have to be a product of your environment." That gave me hope. At 17, I moved out of my mom's house three months shy of graduating high school. I moved in with my aunt and cousin. My aunt stayed on me about my grades because she wanted me to make something out of my life. I went to college during the time I lived with her until she passed away five years later.

I was dating at the time and decided to move in with my then boyfriend and his mom. She is a hardworking woman. She taught me about hard

137

work and dedication. She is the one who encouraged me to join the military instead of working three jobs and going to school. That is where I met my ex-husband. Growing up without my father was hard because I didn't know how a queen was supposed to be treated and loved. I learned from the streets which is never a good learning tool.

So, I had this marriage, but I didn't know how to be a good wife. Then I got pregnant and had my first child. I didn't know what the heck I was doing. I had this child that I had to care for. I had this husband to care for. I learned along the way, but it wasn't easy at all. Not knowing a lot of things put a damper on the marriage and everything else but I survived. The thing that I wished that I had learned earlier from my mom or other role models is how to be a parent and a wife. I had to learn these things the hard way.

From everything that I had gone through in life was life lessons learned. I told myself early in life that I was going to be someone and make something out of my life. I was determined that I was not going to let my past dictate my future or the future of my kids. I may have grown up in challenging circumstances, but I didn't let them ruin me.

I took back my life by living by my own rules. I learned that things will happen in your life, but it is not an option to ever give up. Never give up on yourself. You are never too old to live your dream. I started living my dream of acting and modeling at the age of 45. Never let anyone tell you that you are nothing and that you will never amount to anything. That is a lie. You control your own destiny. I know there will be obstacles or road blocks in the way, but you can climb over those and achieve anything you put your mind to.

Life is about choices. You are not always going to make the right choice, but it is how you handle the situations in your life in the long run that really counts.

ABOUT THE AUTHOR

 Demetria E. Johnson is retired military, actress, model, wife and mother of six (two biological and four step- kids) and grandmother to one with two more on the way.

She is currently a Lead Transportation Assistant at the Naval Weapons Station in Goose Creek, South Carolina. She has a bachelor's degree in Information Systems from the University of

Maryland University College. She works the same job as a civilian that she did in her military career. She retired from the military after 20 years of service. She received many accolades and awards while in the military for her service of helping people.

She has been acting and modeling for the past three years. She has been in independent films like "Angels Revenge" and "I Use 2 Luv Her" and stage productions "For Colored Girls Who Have Considered Suicide When the Rainbow Is Enuf" and "When My Life Changed." She has also modeled in shows like Africstyle Initiatives and CMBEA Fashion Show. She has been receiving rave reviews for her acting and modeling which she loves doing.

Her most recent work, a musical stage play called "When My Life Changed," will debut in March 2019. She was also cast in the mini-series "Life of an OG Cougar" and is preparing for a TV series called "Cycles."

When she isn't working, acting or modeling, she loves spending time with her family: her husband Christopher, kids Freddie, Devon, Shakyra, Taylor, Kennedy, Javin and her granddaughter Riley. She was told that she would not be anything in life, but she defied the odds. Right now, she is living her best life yet.

You can reach her at deemodels8@gmail.com, IG-demi_model_actress, FB-demi johnson/model/actress.

When Darkness Turns to Light

Have you ever had a knowing before you knew the reality of the outcome?

I could feel the flow of movement as I traveled toward the light, but darkness consumed the essences of the light. The noise, the sound of unfamiliar voices and then one I recognized. A new place unknow to my mind but the voice of my mother was right on time. I tried to see this new place as a change from the dark womb that I left but shades of darkness would not let me rest. All I could hear were voices that were rushing to help my mother who they said was dead. The next thing I heard was silence.

Someone had me in their arms as the blanket kept me warm. I was in a new place and I felt displaced. Suddenly, a familiar voice cried out "She is mine!"

According to my mother they thought she had died. The hospital called my father to let him know that he had a daughter, but his wife did not make it. I was told they even took her to the morgue. As God would have it my mother and I met in the elevator. Everyone was talking about the new beautiful baby and when my mother asked to see me, they bent down to show me and she told them I was her baby. Things were sorted out I assume because I ended up where I started -- with my mother. From death to life my journey with my mom was just beginning.

Learning to Function Without Physical Sight

As time went on, I grew, and shades of darkness was the reality of light that I received. Bumping into things became a regular pattern with me. By the time I was one and a half years of age I was diagnosed as blind. Even though I lacked physical eyesight I had a knowing of things that I could not physically see. There was an inner voice that spoke to me and that voice guided me to see even in my shades of natural darkness.

At two years of age I had the most beautiful baby blue bifocals you have ever seen. My inner voice always encouraged me and He became my best friend. My mother would ask me who was I talking to and I would say my friend. Time went by and I entered school. Even though I was visually challenged, the darkness was never a fearful reality because my internal friend would always guide me. Even my classmates knew of my friend. The darkness was only in shades due to the constant comfort of the internal voice that guided me. I learned to trust the inner voice that directed me to safety.

Learning how to walk in a world of light when darkness would appear instantly really took some strategic decision making on my part. I was an adventurous child who was full of curiosity and adventure. I had no idea who or what the inner voice was, but I learned to trust that voice because it stopped me from getting in trouble a whole lot of times.

When Light Silences Darkness

My mother was my mentor and instructor and my dad was my best friend. The instructor knew that beyond my limited sight I was guided by a stronger force. She would always instruct me to learn to listen and not to disobey the inner voice that guided me. She taught me that darkness will only turn to light when the power of the light was absorbed by the listener. The connection of the voice would penetrate the soul to rest in the comfort of the light's instructions. If I attentively listened to the inner voice, I would avoid getting punished or one of those good old lilac bush spankings.

Sometimes my strong will would ignore the inner voice and I reaped the consequences of being stubborn. I learned fast that darkness was a state of consciousness and when you were fortunate to have an inner guide and an instructor/ mother to help you with the interpretation, darkness was no longer an excuse for ignorance. You had to be accountable for what you have internally to work with inside and outside of yourself. The lesson learned was that light can silence darkness when the vessel is yielding to perfect their will to the light and not to the lessor part of self will.

Growing from Evolving Truths

As time continued to unfold, I grew to understand the strong lessons of my mother. She was such an excellent teacher. As a child, she had also heard the inner voice, but she had rejected the lessons it offered. She did not want me to do the same. She knew that the inner voice was my guide and gift. My challenges as a slightly impaired child were individual masterpieces of two lives -- my mother and mine. She could physically see but was not willing to receive the true light of the inner voice to see beyond natural sight. I, on the other hand, was born with a serious sight deficiency but when I was offered the same gift as my mother, she encouraged me to embrace the truths of the inner voice.

My mother knew that my blindness was a gift from God to reach deeper into the gift of true sight whereas I could be a vessel for his glory. My blindness was an invitation to receive abundant light and insight from the Creator of my soul. In the spiritual we know that the soul is the place of decisions. It is where right meets wrong, good meets evil and light meets darkness. My mother engaged my soul to remove the darkness of rejection of truth to receive the gift of eternal life through embracing the inner voice. The inner voice of the spirit of God could and would revive a blind child into a reservoir of light guided by His Divine presence. The transformation of a child without physical sight evolving into a vessel of light.

Learned Lessons to Retain the Light over Darkness

1. Darkness is a state of consciousness that can be overwritten by embracing positive self-worth.

2. Darkness can never swallow the light because light overpowers darkness.

3. Darkness will challenge the light when light refuses to raise its high beams of radiance.

4. Darkness is selected by choice due to the inner rejection of lights beams to inner.

5. Darkness creeps in when hopelessness emerges within.

6. Never romance sorrow because darkness is her companion.

7. Darkness will only satisfy you if you ingest its fumes.

8. Darkness is a choice when the mind flows towards it when the mind is unsettled.

9. Darkness is contagious to a broken soul.

10. Darkness is the vomit of one's sorrow.

My blindness has allowed me to live a rich, full life, guided always by my friend, my inner voice, my Creator. I have learned to trust Him in all things and I am encouraged daily to teach the Word and Truth of God. I am here to empower and help others find their paths through life.

ABOUT THE AUTHOR

Dr. Elizabeth E. Castle is a certified Paracletos Christian counselor, educator, entrepreneur, mother, author, radio and television talk show host, community leader, and most of all a devoted and humble servant of God. She was inspired in 2011 to open a personal counseling service known as "A Deeper You" to assist all persons who desire to achieve wellness of body, mind, and spirit.

Dr. Castle teaches the message of oneness. She strives to empower the whole man in a biblical holistic manner. Through her uplifting radio broadcasts or as an engaging lecturer, she encourages the listener to engage in self-discovery. Though she is challenged with limited natural sight, her inner spiritual sight allows her to empower and help other find their paths through life.

Among her accomplishments, she was honored with a Dr. Martin Luther King full scholarship to the University of Central Florida. She was also the recipient of the first Willie Burton Award. She received her bachelor's degree with high honors from American Intercontinental University with a major in Business Administration with an emphasis in Psychological Disorders. Dr. Castle continued to obtain her master's degree in Education with an emphasis in Curriculum Design.

Dr. Elizabeth E. Castle is a community activist who encourages people to use their unrealized strengths to overcome life challenges. In 2003, under her nonprofit organization, The Agape Resource Collaborative, Inc. (TARC), she established Clean Sweep, which is an inner-city cleanup program. TARC also offered entrepreneurial education and financial literacy programs to communities where she served. Dr. Castle has traveled throughout the country helping community-focused groups to organize and activate community improvement programs such as "Jacob's Ladders," an advocacy program for "at risk youth." An advocate is paired with a youth and their family to achieve educational success.

Dr. Castle has extensively traveled throughout the United States and the West Indies, teaching God's

Word. She spiritually covers churches in Kenya, Nigeria, and Liberia. She has also established churches in Atlanta, Georgia; Sarasota, Florida, and West Palm Beach, Florida, and centers in Charleston, South Carolina and Baltimore, Maryland.

You can reach Dr. Castle via email to dreecastle@yisslearningcenters.com

Visit http://ADeeperU.com for more information on her counseling services.

Visit http://AmazingSpeaks.com for more information on speaker training services.

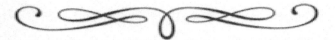

I Recovered From a Broken Heart

Relationships are a vital part of life and finding a good healthy one, where two hearts connect and are in sync with each other, is like finding a hidden golden treasure. Yet many relationships, no matter who the individuals are, can leave one feeling hurt, disappointed and even depressed. Recovering from these feelings is important in order to develop new relationships that can be beneficial to one's personal life.

After many years of wondering if there was a good fit for me, I was so excited to meet a handsome young man I'll call Bobby. To begin, we met through an online dating service, corresponding with each other by email, phone, text, and letters. It was a long-distance relationship; he lived in Texas and I lived in Pennsylvania.

I didn't mind this type of relationship because for many years I lived a very lonely life even though I was active in my community, church and working a full-time job. I must admit having an introverted personality made it very difficult for me to meet the opposite sex and embrace new friends. However, when online dating became popular, I decided to join the club with the persuasion of a few of my girlfriends.

It was easy to care about Bobby because he was good looking, caring and always took time out to talk and listen to me. I began to look forward to our conversations and time together on the phone. His texts to me in the mid-day or his letters that he put so much thought into always brought a smile to my face and literally made my day. I learned to trust Bobby's judgment about many issues I faced in my personal life because whenever I followed his advice I noticed things always worked out for me.

The very first thing that I found amazingly attractive was his voice. Each time I talked with him, it was an energizing and comforting experience just to listen. His voice literally mesmerized me. It was only a matter of time before I developed much passion for him.

After about six months talking over the phone, texting and emailing, we made plans to meet each other face to face. This was a task because we could never agree on how to make it happen. You see, Bobby wanted to come and stay at my house and I felt strongly that we should not stay together on the first visit. "Can you stay in a hotel on our first visit?" I asked. He bluntly refused.

Bobby was a stubborn man. When he made up his mind about something, he never went against it. "I'm coming to Chester to visit you and therefore I want to stay with you. Put me in your guess room and show me some northern hospitality," he said.

"No, I can't do that," I responded.

I could not understand why he did not want to compromise and stay in a hotel on our first visit. Perhaps it was the way I was raised; I thought it would be more appropriate for him to stay in a hotel. When our conversation about him coming to Chester never got anywhere, he invited me to come and stay at his house.

"Ok. You come and stay with me," Bobby said, trying to resolve the issue.

I did not want to stay at his house on our first visit. "I'll stay at a hotel near your place," I informed him.

He was a little resistant at first but reluctantly agreed. We finally had a plan, but every time I planned to travel to Texas, he and I would get in an argument or disagreement and I would end up cancelling my trip. This led to years of visitation delays.

Finally, after four years of waiting, he agreed to come and stay at a hotel in Chester. He made all the arrangements without consulting with me and of course it was on a weekend that did not fit into my schedule. When I dared to mention it to him, he became frustrated and angry. *That was the straw that broke the camel's back.* According to Bobby, he discussed the situation with his older sister and she advised him that I was not serious and his best bet was to move on. He followed her advice and after a few months he sent me an email to report that he was getting married. "I never intended to be single this long," he said, "I want to move on with my life." That was the end for me and I did not try to contact him again.

But I guess we weren't done after all. Four years later July 22, he called and left me a voice message. I will never forget that message. His voice sounded as if he was in distress. "Hi, this is Bobby from Texas. Can you please call me as soon as you can? I need to talk with you."

Of course, I returned his call and we began to talk but this time it was a different conversation. He reported that his wife pulled up a UHAUL truck in front of their house, packed her belongings and left him. He was devastated. I felt drawn by the need to console him. I knew he was married and did not want to get myself involved with a married man. I even prayed with him.

Two of my dearest girlfriends informed me not to talk with him at all. "Let him get support from other places. You should not be the one consoling him." Both agreed.

"He was there for me on many occasions in the past and I want to be there for him," I argued.

After about thirty days, Bobby announced that he was filing for divorce. "Why are you filing for divorce so quickly?" I asked. "You are not giving your wife a chance to reconcile."

"You stay out of my marriage," he responded abruptly. After that I never talked again about his marriage.

We then began to communicate on a regular basis with each other and I slowly developed a deep passion for him once again. We set a date to meet face to face and this time it happened. Two years after that distressful call, he was scheduled to arrive in Philadelphia around 12:35 pm and I was already parked at the airport waiting. I called him on my cell phone. "I'm in a burgundy van." I said.

"I see you," he responded. "I will come to you."

At that moment I was so nervous and yet excited to meet him. I got out of the van to see who was walking toward me and before I could look too long, he was right in front of me. "Bobby," I said as I looked at this man who looked nothing like the pictures I saw. However I did notice the markings around his eyes and knew this was him. He walked up to me and embraced me. I felt a little shy at first because I never met this man who was holding me but I managed to contain myself.

We got inside the van and he began to talk as I drove him to a local hotel. That's when it clicked, I was totally familiar with his voice and it was great! As he talked, I felt like melting.

I must say our time together that weekend was amazing. We went to the movies, we visited Philadelphia and toured the city, we ate dinner together, spent time at the hotel and my house together. We talked and laughed. He called me beautiful and the way he said my name was intoxicating. It felt like I met my perfect match.

Our final day together was on a Sunday. We first attended church, ate lunch and then I drove him to the airport. On the way, he said a few words that were very disturbing. He looked me directly in the eyes, "I'm not ready for a relationship. I am not where you are, so you are going to have to forget me."

I was speechless and dumbfounded! We just had a fabulous weekend together and now he is telling me that I must forget him? I tried to believe it was not true but when he got back to Texas, he slowly faded right out of my life. He would not answer my phone calls or email. If I texted him, occasionally he would text back a word or two but he never initiated any communication with me. I was emotionally crushed because I could do nothing about the distance or separation.

From the very first time I laid eyes on Bobby, I felt love for him. A person may ask me how can you fall in love with someone you never met and only had limited conversations; which were mainly by phone, text, email

153

or letters? Yet when you live a lonely life, that form of communication is a real relationship, at least in my eyes it was. And as quickly as love came, it was gone.

I began to feel overwhelmingly lonely, sad and depressed. I had a friend who noticed my state of being and she said to me, "I don't know what happened to you to cause you to get in this place where you are, but you cannot stay there." That statement made so much sense to me. I had to come out of that place of brokenness.

I remembered an old saying, "It's better to have loved and lost then to have never loved at all." This was my daily affirmation to begin my recovery along with, "I'm going to be alright." I personally would not have ever desired to miss the opportunity to have been in a relationship with Bobby because I learned so much from him and my emotions ran very deep for him like no one else in my life. Yes, my heart was broken and although I was struggling now, I knew eventually I would be alright because I had people in my life who supported me.

How did I recover? These are the seven steps that helped me to overcome a broken heart and I believe they can help you, too.

1. Only talk about the person with one or two trusted friends. Many times we get into the habit of sharing our story with everybody because sometimes we feel talking about it will relieve the pain. Talking to trusted friends who truly know you and your personality may help but talking with too many people will only confuse you with all the different advice you can receive. There will be people who tell you

to call him or her while others advise you not to call at all. This is confusing and sometimes the advice may backfire. People who know you and advised you successfully in the past will be most likely to steer you in the right direction. Limit who you talk to.

2. Don't hate the person for leaving you but rather realize it wasn't meant to be. I know it hurts but you cannot hold onto a person who does not value who you are and does not respond to your needs. How long will you look for a phone call, text, or email and yet receive nothing. And if you are initiating all communications, this is not a true relationship. Apparently, the person feels no commitment to you and sees no benefit in continuing to correspond with you meaning they do not desire a relationship. Remember it may have nothing to do with who you are but rather who they are. Therefore, attempt to let them go without developing anger or bitterness which in turn will only affect you.

    I fell in love with a man who informed me after communicating for more than two years that he was not ready for a relationship and chose to end communication with me. He asked me quite nicely not to call him anymore. I was deeply hurt but continued to call a few times and each conversation left me feeling rejected and sad, so eventually I stopped contacting him completely.

3. After sharing your story about the breakup and processing the fact that the relationship has ended, pick a date to stop talking about him or

her. As long as you talk about the person, you keep that memory alive. It's hard sometimes to face the fact that your beloved is just not into you like that but eventually you will have to stop speaking or reaching out to someone who has pretty much abandoned you. As you stop talking about the person, things will begin to feel different. It's healthy to freely let go and will benefit you in the long run.

4. Get involved with extracurricular activities. Take an exercise, swimming or sewing class. Go dancing, read a good book, volunteer at a local organization or get involved with your church. Do something to keep your mind focused on other things besides a dead relationship.

5. Began to seek out new prospects when you are ready. There's nothing wrong with some time alone. Give your emotions a break and focus on yourself and ways to rebuild your self-esteem. Online dating or being a part of a singles group could be an option for you, but you decide.

6. Use the tools you know best to deal with personal anxiety or stress from the breakup. There are many tools. For example: talking to a counselor or trusted friend; reading, journaling, prayer, mediation, exercise, listening to music, knitting or some other hobby. You know what works best for you!

7. Be true to yourself. Be good to yourself. Love yourself. There is a quote I found that best concludes this list, "Sometimes the best upgrade after a bad relationship isn't falling in

love with another person, it's falling in love with yourself." (author unknown)

ABOUT THE AUTHOR

 JL Coston is a native of Chester, Pennsylvania and founder of Joseph Dreams, Inc., a nonprofit organization serving at-risk populations. She holds a BSN from Howard University and MTS from Eastern Baptist Theological Seminary. She was voted 1988 Nurse of Hope for the American Cancer Society in Delaware County, Pa. and served as a Medical Missionary to Kingston, Jamaica.

Her service to the local church included her involvement with Hospital and Nursing Home Ministries, Prayer Ministry and Neighborhood Evangelistic Teams. She is the author of "A Portrait of Mommy, Expressions of Love, Faith, and Perseverance" and "Escape to Pray!"

Contact: JL Coston on Facebook
        Email: aportraitofmommy@gmail.com
        Phone: 484-478-1989

Website: *https://www.aportraitofmommy.com*

From Grief to Growth

JOURNAL NOTE:

Through the last 2-years, I've learned a painful lesson. We go through life making plans and God makes the final decision. My husband of 28 years, William, the father of my children - died suddenly of a heart attack – in his sleep. He was only 52-years-old. My world changed. Our family will never be the same ever again.

While in mourning, feelings of grief and sorrow and overwhelming loss was ever-present. I felt numb, shocked and fearful. I felt guilty for not seeing signs or thinking that perhaps I could've done something ... anything for William to be healthier ... live longer. We had made plans in our quest to retire early. At some point, I may have even felt angry at him for leaving us. All these feelings, I later learned, are normal. There are no rules about how you should feel. There is no right or wrong way to mourn the loss of a loved one – or to grieve for the life you once had.

Eventually, I learned that when I grieve, I can feel both physical and emotional pain. In addition, some people can also have the following, like I did:

> *Trouble sleeping*
> *Little interest in food*
> *Problems with concentration*
> *A hard time making decision*

When grieving, I dealt with feelings of loss, but I know that I must also put my own life back together. This is going to be hard work. I've been told that as time passes, I will still miss William, but I will have joy and laugh again. I was told that the intense pain lessens as you travel through the grief recovery process. There will be good and bad days. I will know that I am healing, feeling better, when the good days begin to outnumber the bad days.

****

I'm the only daughter and oldest of three children born to James and Carrie Smalls. My brothers Darryl and James, along with my dad, were the first men to love me unconditionally. I learned early in life to be responsible, focused, independent, and to get an education. To be the leader of my own life. To help pay for college, I joined the Army as an enlisted soldier and through training and education became a Finance Officer and Public Affairs Officer with the rank of Captain. Combined with my Army Reserve, National Guard, and brief active duty assignment during Operation Desert Storm, I served in the military for 18 years.

On the way to Army Basic Training (Ft. Jackson, South Carolina), I met my husband William (a New Yorker from the Bronx), who also joined as an enlisted soldier and later became an Army officer.

After our military careers, William and I held positions in both non-profits and the local school systems as we built a life together and raised our two sons, William II and Matthew, both of whom later became Army veterans as well. On May 16, 2016, our life changed in a way that I never expected. My husband of 28 years, then a middle school Assistant Principal, passed away in his sleep on a Monday from a fatal heart attack. He was a devoted husband and loving father. The world as I knew it would never be the same. When you experience the trauma of a life-changing event, you wonder: "How can the world go on when my family's world is falling apart?"

From Summer 2016 through the Fall of 2018, I busied myself grieving through my new roles as a widow, empty nester, and former school principal. I decided it was time to leave education (after 22 years) as I believed that God gave me gifts and talents to do many things in life, and to use them in fulfilling ways to serve others in a new role. I wanted to continue to uplift and inspire others as I navigated through my own journey.

To do that, I knew I needed to be in a different environment, one that had fewer memories of the life we built together. It was too painful being in the house we raised a family in or driving down the streets that held memories of driving to work and our date nights. We had careers and close friends in Georgia, but no family where we lived. So, I resigned to take effect at the end of my contract year in June 2017 with the school system, prepared to downsize and sell our family home, and relocate to a place I've never lived – but did have family.

I relocated from Georgia to South Carolina and avoided constant grieving by staying busy (to numb the hurt and loneliness), getting settled, and paving a new path for myself to travel alone. This was going to be a major transition. Within a year, my sons also relocated to progress in their lives in other states. A new start for the three of us that we now call our family, our "new normal."

During this time, I learned to be flexible. To ask for advice or help. Family and friends continued to pray for us and encourage us. I thought often about who am I if I'm no longer a wife, a mother raising children, a school principal? How will I transform and redesign my life now that I've chosen to travel down a new path as a single woman in mid-life – creating an encore career as an entrepreneur? I need to create a new network in a new state. I need to travel a new path in this journey called life. Can I do it? Is it too late to strengthen my resilience, and transition strong enough to transform myself? Can I experience joy on the other side of mourning? I must. I have family and friends whom I love, and who love me.

I decided I am resilient. So now what? I decided to tie up my boots for the journey, take action, and get ready to make a breakthrough! I needed to figure out a way to strengthen my resilience muscle to make the rest of my life the best of my life and do it one day at a time. My sons need their mom. I needed my sons to see that the one constant in life is change. But if you create a plan, you must actively work the plan. God's purpose for us will reveal itself because there's more He has for us to do.

So, with that revelation, I decided to name my company Boots to Breakthrough LLC. The name reminds me that whatever we're going through (transition/trauma/tragedy), it's important to take time to become well and strengthen your resilience (your boots/plan), actively put it in place (tie it up), so you can create the foundation you'll need to achieve momentum and make your breakthrough. That's what I did through participating in two grief recovery groups and researching wellness and resiliency.

As a result, I learned about the Dimensions of Wellness and it has enriched my life and is the foundation of the services I provide through Boots to Breakthrough.

Through my own transition, I learned that at one time or another, an estimated 80% of people experience a life-altering traumatic event, and most grow stronger from surviving, according to decades of research by leading institutions like Harvard and Yale universities and the University of Pennsylvania. We can prepare now for life's inevitable challenges and setbacks – and make a comeback – by developing the skills and tools of resilience.

I learned the hopeful message that it's possible to go through the most terrible things, and still get through to a better place. Researchers have found that, like elastic stretched beyond its normal limits, people often don't just bounce back to their old form but stretch and expand in new ways.

According to many studies, 60-80 percent of people grow in some way from personal trauma, known as "post-traumatic growth," according to David B. Feldman, Associate Professor of counseling psychology at California's Santa Clara University and co-author with Lee Daniel Kravetz of ***Supersurvivors: The Surprising Link Between Suffering and Success***. "Post-traumatic growth can be as simple as appreciating each day more. It can mean deepening relationships. It may result in a renewed sense of spirituality. Or, it might take one's life in a dramatically different direction," says Feldman. This has been my experience.

163

I want to encourage others going through life transitions, whether it's in their journey through spiritual growth and mindfulness, physical health, emotional well-being, environmental comfort, restructuring social relationships (professional and personal), learning and growing intellectually, feeling fulfilled in your occupation, or becoming financially fit – that you can do it. If you can imagine it, you can dream it, if you can dream it – you can become it. Life is a journey and you can determine the path that you will take to enjoy the journey along the way to your new destination.

No one ever said that life was easy. Choosing to be self-directed instead of stumbling in self-pity in the face of challenges, differentiates those that thrive from those who merely survive. It's important to take responsibility for your life and manage the way you want to live it. We all have choices as to the road we will travel in the journey of life, even in the face of difficulty.

In retrospect, personally, I wish I had known more about being "present" in my life.

Like many women, I did strive for work-life balance – to juggle as much as I could and then later, I would plan to enjoy life more. I realize even more now that there is no real work-life balance – there's just life. I wish I had spent more moments being in the moment. I thought William and I had more time left to freely enjoy the fruits of our labor and sacrifices in an early retirement life together. I imagined we had more time to enjoy our sons becoming men and creating their own paths. He was my best friend and sometimes, my most ardent cheerleader. Looking back, I realize that he probably made a lot of sacrifices through his patience with my pursuits and community involvements. It wasn't always easy. I can think of at least three times where we could've divorced because either of us did not feel like a priority in the other person's life.

Through the years, I was so focused on my "destinations" (positions and achievements) in life that I didn't balance my life and work through this journey along the way. I thought that with our accomplishments, our careers, our desire to start a business, and enjoy our empty nest ... we were still young enough to enjoy more exciting years before us. William was always telling me to "slow down", "calm down", "take time to relax." I was driven, ambitious, and felt we had lots of time left to "slow down" later. I wish I had realized earlier in life to not to be so busy "making a living," that I lost sight of "living my life." The past is gone, tomorrow is not promised, and our present – this moment in time – the present is a "gift." The present is the only real time we have any control over.

Once I decided to resign early from education, while painfully navigating through my first two years of my grief process, it became clear that my biggest challenge was to travel through the fog of despair in my personal and professional life. I needed to become 'unstuck' and see clearly through my tears and tie up my boots, prepare for this new journey and start my hike towards a breakthrough for my sons and I as we moved forward in life. Like military training road marches, you know you must go the distance and you must make it to the other side – you've got a mission to accomplish.

Through my transition journey to transformation, I demonstrate to others that obstacles and challenges don't define you. You must have a growth mindset focusing on your strengths and identifying those areas that you need to set goals to act and improve upon. Having a balanced, yet positive outlook that's realistic enables you to move on from trauma according to Doug Hensch, author of ***Positively Resilient: 5-1/2 Secrets to Beat Stress, Overcome Obstacles, and Defeat Anxiety.*** Hensch also found that being pragmatic serves you far better than a false sense of optimism about bad situations, that "you experience grieving the loss, but think realistically about what to do next. Optimism in the best sense is focusing on the positive without denying the negative, while focusing on what's in your control," notes Hensch.

To transition through grief and transform my life in the wake of our family's painful "new normal" of life without my husband whom I spent half of my life with, I felt pursuing entrepreneurialism was a dream that we shared. There were emotional obstacles in moving forward: resigning from the school system after a career of 22-years; preparing for and selling our Georgia home; downsizing and relocating to a South Carolina townhouse; helping my sons prepare and relocate to Colorado and Maryland; starting a new career as an entrepreneur and creating a new professional network in South Carolina; avoiding grief recovery during the first 1-1/2 years. All of these kept me busy enough to unsuccessfully deal with the grief (avoidance). Once I began to work through my grief, the fog began to clear and what were once obstacles became stepping stones to begin the journey of redesigning my life in 2018.

Having a purpose is a huge indicator of whether a person will rise to the occasion of overcoming an obstacle. You can endure almost anything if you have a mission or believe that what you are doing has meaning. It gives you more strength. As I began to process through how much my life has changed with my husband's sudden fatal heart attack at home, I could've descended into a deep depression and given up. Or, I could focus on the love we shared for one another, get into a grief recovery group or therapy, and make a difference by inspiring, encouraging, and helping others whom are going through a life transition.

In my transition and grief recovery process, I researched strategies that I could use to transform and redesign my life. I wanted to strengthen my resilience and eventually experience joy – and see the sun rise again on the other side of mourning. I found research about the Dimensions of Wellness (1976) by Dr. Bill Hettler, Co-Founder of the National Wellness Institute. "Wellness" is oftentimes thought of in terms of physical health only. The word invokes thoughts of nutrition, exercise, weight management, blood pressure, etc. Wellness, however, is much more than physical health. Wellness is a full integration of physical, mental and spiritual well-being. It is a complex interaction that leads to quality of life and strengthening your resiliency.

Wellness is commonly viewed as having six dimensions and has expanded to eight dimensions in living a full and holistic life. Each dimension contributes to my own sense of wellness or quality of life, and each may affect and/or overlap the others. I've experienced that at times one dimension may be more prominent than others, but neglect of any one dimension for any length of time can have an adverse effect on overall quality of life. The 8 Dimensions of Wellness are: Spiritual, Physical, Emotional, Environmental, Social (relationships), Intellectual (life-long learning), Occupational, and Financial.

Spiritual Wellness is the ability to establish peace and harmony in our lives. The ability to develop congruency between values and actions.

Physical Wellness is the ability to maintain a healthy quality of life that allows us to get through our daily activities without undue fatigue or physical stress.

Emotional Wellness is the ability to understand ourselves and cope with the challenges life can bring. The ability to acknowledge and share feelings of anger, fear, sadness or stress; hope, love, joy and happiness in a productive.

Environmental Wellness is the ability to recognize our own responsibility for the quality of the air, the water and the land that surrounds us. The ability to make a positive impact on the quality of our environment, be it our homes, our communities or our planet.

Social Wellness is the ability to relate to and connect with other people in our world. Our ability to establish and maintain positive relationships with family, friends and co-workers.

Intellectual Wellness is the desire to learn new concepts, improve skills and seek challenges in pursuit of lifelong learning.

Occupational Wellness is the ability to get personal fulfillment from our jobs or chosen career fields while still maintaining balance in our lives. Incorporated here also is financial wellness, a feeling of satisfaction about your financial situation.

Financial Wellness involves the ability to have financial resources to meet practical needs, and a sense of control and knowledge about personal finances.

I realized that like myself, many people, both civilian and military, undergo various types of transition in their life and could benefit from a strategic approach through which to set goals in their life.

In March 2018, I began Boots to Breakthrough LLC, as a Transition Strategist to coach, inspire, and encourage people to become more resilient, set goals through strategies within the Dimensions of Wellness, and live their best life. Boots to Breakthrough was awarded a 2018 SCORE Veteran's Business Grant, was a finalist for the Women Veterans Alliance-2018 Melissa Washington Small Business Award, and I became a Resiliency Facilitator for the American Red Cross. As a Resiliency Facilitator, I conduct Reconnection Workshops to support and assist service members and their families in dealing with the issues and challenges of returning home from deployments; and for the veteran, reintegration back into their civilian community.

I know firsthand about making plans, transitioning, and redesigning my life's purpose when life as you knew it is forever changed. My purpose is to inspire others at the transitional pathways of their lives. In my new hometown South Carolina, Mayor John Tecklenburg of Charleston appointed me as a Commissioner to his *Commission on Homelessness and Affordable Housing*. I also serve on the advisory board for the *Vantage Point Foundation*, which guides post 9/11 veterans who experienced wartime trauma and their families to healing and civilian success.

One may wonder what the future could possibly hold for me? My life was shaped by my husband's companionship, advice, protection, and love. There was a sense of security that I lost when William passed away. Healing for my sons and I came through engaging in activities, building relationships, and finding things we enjoy doing. Through my local and national speaking engagements, workshops, online learning, retreats, and consultant work, I love my evolved role as a Transition Strategist working with people to transform their lives through their transition. I bring a veteran's leadership, a mother's compassion, a widow's heart and professional knowledge to any endeavor in which I am involved.

As my parents' eldest child, raised in the inner city of New York, Captain in the Army, served as a military spouse, mother of sons whom are veterans, educator, widow, and entrepreneur – I am a woman who's living a life of many transitions! I've used all my experiences to develop personally, grow professionally, and improve my overall well-being. I am purposeful about using my experiences, gifts and talents to be of service.

So, I am here to tell you that if I can do it, you can do it too! It's never too late to become more of who you are - resilient or ready to seize the moment! Every day is a fresh start to do what makes your heart leap! And perhaps most importantly, YOU CAN experience joy on the other side of mourning. Grief is a process. Grief and mourning is a reflection of your love. With encouraging support, you can embrace loving your life and experience joy in the new you.

Time to strap up your boots (create a plan and prepare to travel) and make a breakthrough to the destiny that awaits you!

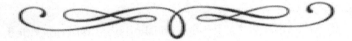

ABOUT THE AUTHOR

Dr. Ja'net Bishop, Ed.D is a Transition Strategist, Speaker, Author, Consultant and owner of Boots to Breakthrough LLC.

She launched her military spouse coaching/training program, "Mission: I Am Possible," and is excited that the Vantage Point Foundation has considered embracing the research-based 8 Dimensions of Wellness as a framework for their program's services!

Ja'net serves on the Executive Board of the National Alternative Education Association advocating for alternative schools in the United States. As of December 2018, she was inducted as a Board Member for the YMCA (Metro-Charleston, SC). She is a member of ROTARY-Historic Charleston, and the Charleston Chapters of the American Business Women's Association (ABWA) and the National Women Veterans of America and involved in various community service efforts.

She gives God the praise for His grace, mercy, and favor for ordering her steps along this journey. She knows that with the blessings that have occurred, she is doing His will.

In December 2014, Ja'net published her first book titled, ***How Much Joy is in Your Journey: A Creative Guide to Your Fearless Vision*** available on Amazon. This book reignited her desire to transform life through mid-life and career transition and to remember joy in the process. As an author and advocate for women empowerment, in 2019 she anticipates publishing a gratitude journal and a book chronicling her 2-year transformation through the 8 Dimensions of Wellness as she redesigned her life in those areas.

Ja'net can reached:

URL: www.BootstoBreakthrough.com
Work: (762) 233-1118
Email: dr.janet.bishop@gmail.com
FACEBOOK: Ja'net Bishop
FACEBOOK: Boots to Breakthrough
LinkedIn: Dr. Ja'net Bishop

■■■

Helpful Resilience Resources:

From We to Me: Embracing Life Again After The Death or Divorce of a Spouse, by Susan J. Zonnebelt-Smeenge, RN, Ed.D and Robert C. De Vries, DMin., PhD

Option B: Facing Adversity, Building Resilience, and Finding Joy, by Sheryl Sandberg & Adam Grant

OptionB.org provides supportive space online for survivors of trauma and adversity to share stories, connect with others and get help from experts.

Griefshare.com provides friendly, caring group of people who will walk alongside you through one of life's most difficult experiences. You don't have to go through the grieving process alone.

****

(Adapted from autobiographical article featured in *Focus on Fabulous Magazine's* December 2018 issue)

Other Books & Publications by our Contributors

God, are you listening? Hearing His voice through forgiveness & faith, c. michelle bryant

In an Instant, c. michelle bryant

Rambling Roads, a collection of thoughts, poems and prayers, c. michelle Bryant

Walking in my mind, a journey with words, c. michelle Bryant

Ten effective ways to Rise Up, Aim High, Stand Tall & Be Outstanding in the field of life & business, c. michelle Bryant

Focus on Fabulous Magazine, More Than a Magazine ... An Experience, a quarterly publication edited and published by c. michelle bryant, http://FofMagazine.com

My Truth, Enduring Death on Many Levels, Kimberly Mills

The Small Business Owner's Tax Guide: what every small business owner must know about reducing taxes, Katryna Johnson, J.D.

Killer Marketing Strategies, Katryna Johnson, J.D.

How Much Joy is in Your Journey? A Creative Guide to Your Fearless Vision, Dr. Ja'net Bishop

A Portrait of Mommy, JL Coston

Altered On Impact, From Trauma to Transformation: How a Traumatic Brain Injury Taught Me to Lead a Purposeful Life, Lynn DelGaudio

Coming soon!

Books by c michelle Bryant, Camilla Herold, and Dr. Ja'net Bishop, Katryna Johnson

IF YOU ENJOYED THIS BOOK

PLEASE LEAVE A

5-STAR REVIEW ON

AMAZON.COM

If you have been touched, moved, inspired or encouraged by a story or stories in this book, please reach out to the author(s) and let them know. Your feedback means a lot.

Thank you!

Do you have a story to share?

A new edition of ***If She Can...
Inspiring Stories of Grit, Hope
and Courage*** will be accepting
submissions soon.

Visit **IfSheCan.com** for more
information.

More about Mirelli Entrepreneur Training for Women

Mirelli is a business solution for women in business. With training, support and guidance, you CAN live the life of your dreams.

Mirelli provides:

- One-on-one Coaching (in-person and virtual)
- Networking
- DIY Online Training Library
- Workshops & Webinars
- Marketing & Promotion Support
- Daily Motivation
- Weekly Newsletter
- Supportive and Collaborative Community
- Affordable monthly membership fees

Check out our membership options at

Mirellietc.com/Join-Now

Made in the USA
Columbia, SC
08 April 2019